# UNSHATTERED BRAVE WOMAN

## EIGHT DECADES OF TURBULENCE DEFEATED WITH INTREPID SMILE

GANGU SUBBAYYA

*"I lost my children now the whole world's children are my children"*

*—Gangu Subbayya*

# Contents

# Contents

# Author's Note

Life is a unique journey of tales. Each human has its own story, some have wonderful while some make it wonderful. It's a matter of bravery; some lead their own while some give their power to someone else. The journey which I have been drafting has taught me to be rebellious with boundaries. Bravery is not always fighting but bravery is to build patience with a smile. Gangu has been my inspiration and I am sure with this book she would be the inspiration for many. The journey of eight decades needs series especially when the contribution is beyond the limits. Each phase of her life has so much to learn. A woman who creates smiles and tears of happiness. What the world would say? When the darkness is turned into brightness. When a hope turned into reality. With Gangu many have witnessed them. Let's take a glimpse into a journey that is full of emotions, learning and motivation.

# Foreword

Unshattered brave woman stands alone to deliver what it takes to deliver. She walks alone to walk the talk and brings the unfinished to its fruition, drawing strength from the subtle powers of her inner self. She accepts deep faith, reassuring hope and love unconditional as the life unfolds in manifold ways in its nano seconds. Overwhelmed or shattered she becomes, in life's quintessential play! As the seasons of life unfolds, the eventful heartbreaks that falls on her, one after the other, she survives and transforms herself as a radiant warrior: triggering a spiritual metamorphosis.

Radiant woman warrior like Gangu Subbayya, through the spiritual metamorphosis, survives the onslaught of crushing life events, existential probing and even self-doubts. She receives her convincing answers from the reservoirs of inner self that couch the thorny and stoney paths. From the numerous gullies of life, thus she embarks the highway of consciousness.

Now immersed in the deep universal consciousness of becoming, she shines as a true warrior that defines the spirit of unshattered brave woman. In our modern world, especially in India, living as a woman survivor warrior is remarkable. She knows how to use her strength and is courageous to move forward regardless of the circumstances. Unlike others she stands up for herself and for others. She challenges the status quo and creates armies that change the world. She brings a warrior approach to the place wherever she is living and breathes life to others.

I sincerely trust, this book titled as 'Unshattered Brave Woman' by Gangu Subbayya would enlighten us to what it takes to stand alone as a great human being! Let us prepare ourselves to become the one who is open to become the bravest as we immerse ourselves with her untold stories of adventures and unimaginable life narratives in its original spirit. May the blessings of life embrace us as the journey begins...lovingly and peacefully...

**Brother Joseph Sebastian**
**In charge**
**Welfare Society for Destitute Children**
**St.Catherine of Siena**
**Mumbai**

# CHAPTER ONE

# Golden period– childhood

In the era of World War II, the world was unrest while India was under the colonial rule of the Britishers. The voice of freedom was taking its peak singing the rebellious song of independence. Freedom from slavery every Indian's heart yearned loud. On December 5th, 1940, a brave girl, Gangu, begins her journey through turmoil in the small, beautiful town of Madikeri, Karnataka, popularly known as Mini Switzerland in the 90's. Those mesmerising hilly mountains Madikeri of are breathtaking for nature lovers.

The little Kodagu hamlet erupted in an exuberant celebration with the infant's arrival. Gangu, a small wonder born one month early, had been born prematurely. It was a day of unprecedented joy for everyone as the community came to celebrate the joyous event of the daughter's arrival. Unfortunately, the hope of her survival was low as there were no incubators at that time. The weather was cold it was winter. Luckily her grandmother would warm water and keep it in the bottle around her. That's how her journey begins with struggle.

Gangu was a beautiful and joyous child, and her innocence made her the most beloved by everyone who knew her. Her round, brilliant face resembled the luminous moon, giving a soothing light that attracted everyone. Her eyes, like glittering stars in the night sky, gleamed with a fascinating brilliance, framed by long, thick eyelashes that further added to their allure. Her cheeks, coloured with a subtle flush, were as smooth and gentle as rose petals, calling for tender caresses. Her flawless pink lips contrasted well with her light, almost porcelain-like skin, rounding off her angelic look.

Gangu spent her early childhood days when the struggle for independence was at its peak. One of her most distinct recollections is of the momentous day India earned freedom. She recalls how the Indian flag was proudly flown on practically every house in her area. Young Gangu was inspired by the sight of the brilliant tricolour flying in the air. She couldn't even begin to convey the scale of the flag, which appeared so huge and gorgeous to her. The palpable sense of pride, joy, and solidarity imprinted her little heart, representing hope and perseverance.

Before the independence of India, a tragic event took place in Gangu's life. The little princess went on searching for her dad, holding a tiny piece of paper door to door, asking everyone in the locality about her father. Gangu's father was a doctor by profession; his name was B.K. Subbayya. He was a skilled doctor with a good number of years of experience in the medical field; therefore, he was appointed by the British government to serve the injured soldiers on the battlefield during the Second World War. Communicating the message was not at all easy at the time. It would take months to send a few words of message to dear ones.

One day, suddenly, a rumour grew that spread all over the locality as a fire that Gangu's father had died. Gangu's mother, Sita, has a family-oriented personality. A river of love is not half; she has an ocean of love for her family. Sweet, kind young woman with lots of courage. As this rumour reached Gangu's mother, it made her emotional. She burst out badly with tears flowing from her eyes. Little child Gangu was sitting with her innocent, puzzled face, watching this all from a corner.

After the breakdown, the first word Gangu's mother says, I know he is alive and will return soon! She repeats this almost three or four times.

Soon after that she says, he has only lost the connection to communicating with us. He is alright; he will come back.

The women all around repeatedly said, No, he died! He will not come back; he has left the world. They asked her to wear an eye-flashing white saree for his soul to rest in peace and condolence. Angelic Gangu was helpless. As days passed and the war came to an end with the defeat of the Nazis, Gangu's father came back. Gangu's mother's hope has won. He was alive and had returned home safely, back to his family. It was a day of enjoyment for the entire family, and Gangu's family was complete again.

While growing up, she turned out to be clever and notorious. She was the only daughter and she had one brother. Therefore, was pampered the most. Gangu has a good bond with her parents; her father is like a 'God' to her and her mother is a best friend. She has no secrets; everything that happened to her is known to her mother. Loved her brother most.

Gangu was endowed not just with beauty and purity, but also with money as well as high status in society. Gangu's father, a powerful and influential man, made certain that she had all she needed. She lived in a luxurious bungalow, surrounded by the best comforts money could buy. Despite her privileged background, Gangu was humble and kind-hearted, endearing herself to everyone she encountered. Her father's status gave her several benefits, but it was her natural charm and kindness that made her liked. Gangu's life was a perfect combination of richness and simplicity, enchanting everyone who crossed her way.

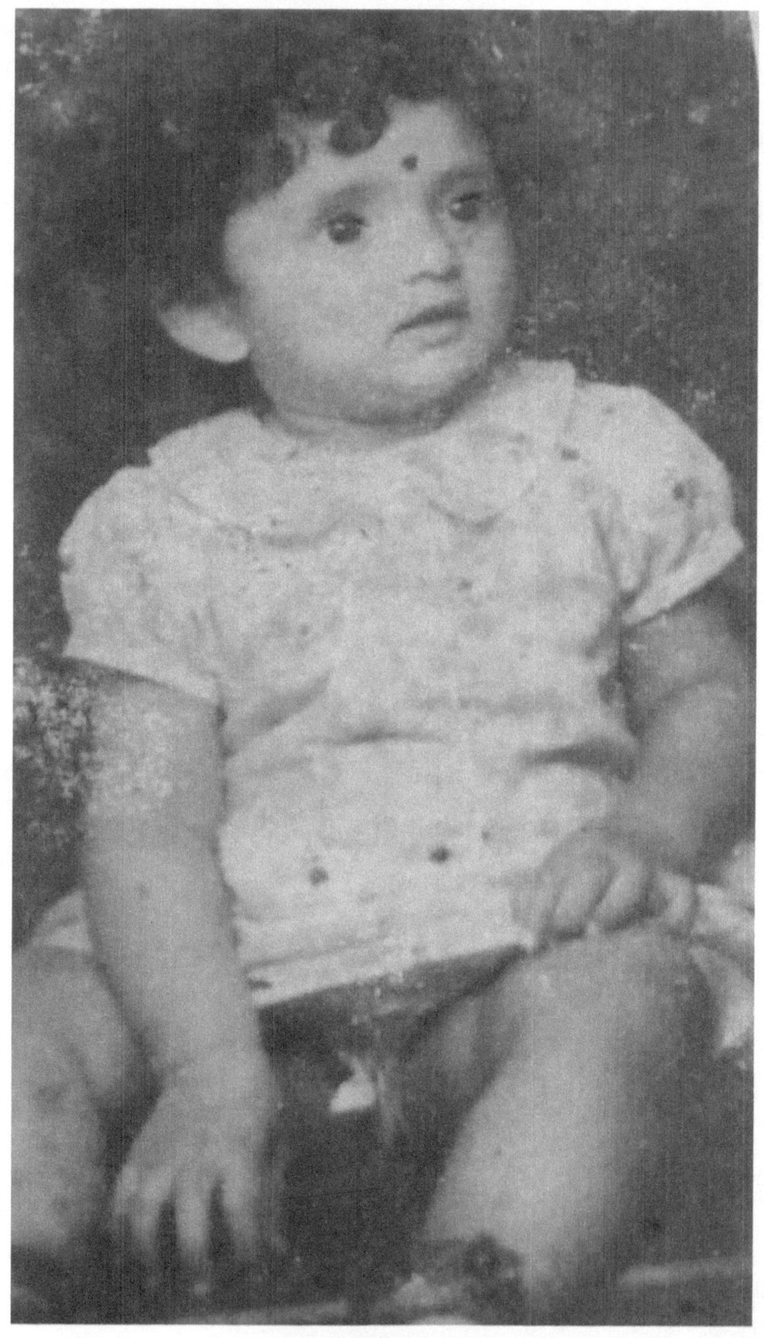

*Gangu 10 months old*

***'Gangu always says, childhood for me is a golden period of life'***
Childhood has little to think about but more to enjoy. Except for the incident when her father went missing, she doesn't like to recall it. Deep within the emerald embrace of Kodagu's hills resides the Kodagu community, to which Gangu belongs, a lineage of warriors forged by the mountain winds. Their ancestry whispers of battles fought and lands protected, a legacy etched in the calloused hands that now hold not just weapons but the deeds of a rich inheritance.

The Kodagu men, descendants of a proud line, are drawn to the call of duty. Their valour echoes through generations, a testament to the spirit that courses through their veins. These are the inheritors of the hills, protectors by birthright, and stewards of a legacy as vast and verdant as the Kodagu landscape itself. Theirs is a story woven with threads of courage, tradition, and the unwavering resolve of a warrior people.

Puthari erupts as the Kodagu Hills become golden in the fall. This harvest celebration, held in November or December, is overflowing with thankfulness. Consider fields blazing with gold, brimming baskets, and jubilation's rhythmic thrum. Puthari is a vivid tapestry woven with gratitude for the earth's richness, laughter booming through the fresh air, and the Kodagu community joining in triumphant feasting.

Gangu was a talented person from childhood. She was average in academics but excelled in extracurricular activities. She had an immense fondness for singing and dancing, and her performances frequently wowed people around her. Gangu, in addition to her creative abilities, was passionate about stitching and knitting, which she spent hours mastering. Despite her early desire to be a doctor, she attended Mysore University and earned a Bachelor of Arts degree. Gangu and her younger brother, Nanda, had a special relationship, and she would often take him with her. She was like a second mother to him, loving and caring for him with unshakable passion. Their tight bond was a special part of her life.

Conformity felt like a suffocating cloak from a young age. She wasn't built for following well-worn paths, a rebellious spirit crackled within her, yearning to blaze her trail. The world outside felt like a boundless sky, a canvas waiting for her to paint her masterpiece of success. Limitations were mere whispers to her, drowned out by the roar of her ambition. She craved the thrill of the unknown, the satisfaction of pushing boundaries, just like a fledgling bird desperately yearning to take flight. As she grew, this revolutionary spirit only intensified. Success wasn't a destination, but a boundless journey, a horizon she was determined to reach with every beat of her ambitious wings.

# CHAPTER TWO

# Teenage Bucket— Age of Change

For Gangu, a teenager is a bucket of fun memories. She was enthusiastic about exploring new things and flying high to limitless boundaries. She often used to spend her vacations in her native place located remotely in Mysore. Greenery, high mountains touching the sky, a clear river with a smooth sound of calming mind, birds rhyming voices of enjoyment, and narrow unpaved streets were all that she could find in her native place. Whenever they commuted, four of the servants would come to pick them up sent by Gangu's grandfather. Her paternal grandfather has a pleasing personality—a handsome, fair complexion and blue gem eyes with tinted red checks. While her paternal grandmother made a heavenly journey, she was named Gangu after her.

Gangu has been staying in the city and would not love to visit the native place due to the lack of facilities. There were no toilets, poor water facilities, a lack of sanitation, and poor infrastructure. There was ample space in the bungalow and a grand backyard but Gangu did not like the place at all. At last, they told their grandfather they did not like the place and would never come here again. If you want to meet us come to our place. After that, Gangu did not go to her native place again, but her brother used to go.

Gangu was timid and notorious. Till the seventh grade, Gangu studied at co-education after the seventh grade the boys and girls were separated. Before that, they used to giggle together and enjoy making unforgettable memories. The boys would have pockets full of fruits. While the girls were as clever as always, they sharply took away their fruits, leaving the boys nothing to eat.

During this journey, she met her lifelong friend. She was the dearest they were partners in crime. Gangu and she would spend the entire day together. They would go to movies and parks. They also play different games together.

Every Indian woman has tied the saree once in a lifetime. Many girls grow up playing by draping a dupatta into a saree. Once the little girl, Gangu did the same. She was in her early teens. The Kodagu community drapes the saree differently instead of taking the pallu (the end of the saree) from the front they take the pallu from the back. Beautifully draped saree in the traditional way like her community Gangu when in front of her father, whom she calls 'pappa'

Running straight to Pappa Gangu told, Pappa, tell me how I am looking. She said it twice.

Her father looked at her once and turned his head down.

And keep on repeating, Go from here! Go from here! Go from here!

Gangu moved a bit far from her father.

Her father said, My daughter has grown up. One day I have to get her married and apart my piece of heart away. Being emotional with tears in his eyes

Narrating to her mother.

Gangu's mischief was on the next level. Different from the world since the early days. She was attracted to her maternal grandmother. She was kind, sweet lady who was only 29 years old when she lost her husband and raised her two daughters by herself all alone. Gangu would admire her and spending time with her was lots of time with joy.

She would say to her mother, You are nowhere near my grandmother. The qualities of her grandmother have a print on her heart.

Once her father went to a conference in Bombay leaving them behind at the grandmother's house. Gangu was on top of the world to be at the grandmother's place. Guess what her notaries evil wake up. Her mother asked her to get something for the town which was not too far from her grandmother's house. Since their women were not allowed to go out after the age of twelve or thirteen. Her mother has never seen the market in her lifetime. If she wanted to buy something the shop would come to their home carrying a huge trunk of clothes, jewellery and so on. Listening to her mother's instructions Gangu went to buy from the town. While going back, she found something mysterious.

When running to the house and telling the mother, You know a man is hanging on the tree.

Listening to Gangu, her mother, grandmothers, servants, and other family members ran towards the tree. The distance between the spot and the house was more than one kilometre. Sunlight was harsh at that time. There was a huge scarecrow near the tree and nothing else.

When reaching there Gangu started screaming, it was a prank. April fool! The bashing she got from her mother was unspeakable and she learned a lifelong lesson. The naughty girl with a good heart.

As growing up Gangu turned out to be mature. It was this phase where she was mentally unstable because of her physical appearance. Due to injury, she was not able to exercise and therefore she gained a lot of weight and her skin turned dusky. Been in a country like India where the definition of beauty is fair sparkling skin tone and slim body shape. Nobody would care about your health conditions. This sudden change upsets Gangu.

**‘Everyone would say, she turned so dark and looked so ugly’**

This was a phrase she heard frequently from numerous individuals. However, there was one aunty who would often remark, "Wait, as she grows, she will become beautiful." These statements, while maybe intended to be reassuring, had a detrimental effect on her. Because of this continuous statement, she began to shun social events, feeling self-conscious and uneasy in social situations. She gradually began to isolate herself, preferring the privacy of her own company to the potential scrutiny of others. The dread of the judgement, along with the weight of these remarks, caused her to retreat from the social engagements she formerly loved.

**Gangu dancing—Shiv Tandav Nritya**

One day her father asked her to get ready. We are going out for an event. Gangu just burst out with tears saying, I don't want to go anywhere.

Her father consoled her with affection and asked, Why are you doing that, dear?

Tears in her eyes Gangu spoke, I don't like to let people speak about my appearance.

You look like you have gained weight and turned dusky are common remarks in gatherings.

You all look so perfect with a fair complexion. I am nowhere close to you.

I look so ugly duckling.

After a few days, she started getting sick with a high temperature. Once a week she would get a high fever. Her mother understood and thought that her health was deteriorating due to harsh remarks. The maternal impulses of her mother surged. Racked with a powerful combination of love and righteous wrath, she silently vowed to herself that no one would ever again diminish her daughter's value by making careless remarks about how she looked. Gangu felt a new confidence developing inside her, knowing that she was loved and adored just as she was, as she observed her mother's unwavering support. The time came when Gangu turned seventeen, it was a 360-degree change, extremely beautiful, curly shoulder-length hair, broad glittering eyes and thin body type. She would get several marriage proposals. Out of affection, her mother burst into tears saying, My daughter is just seventeen let her study.

She had a special link with her father and mother, which she treasured dearly. Her father was overprotective, often acting as a barrier to protect her from danger. He was her constant guardian, making sure she felt safe and protected at all times. Her mother, on the other hand, was caring by nature and assured no trouble ever touched her. Her mother's soft temperament offered a reassuring presence, establishing a harmonic mix of protection and caring. Her parents established a solid support system around her, surrounding her with love, safety, and warmth.

# CHAPTER THREE

# College Memories

The memories which Gangu collects from the golden days were an epic of a series. One such memory is the trip from college. It was not a piece of cake to get permission for the journey. Gangu has mastered the skill of persuading so she did.

She persuaded the Father by being emotional by saying, please let me go. I want to explore!

Gangu assured her father by saying, I will take care of myself and as guided by mother I will stay away from boys one arm's length.

Pappa, some professors will take care of us. Don't worry! Gangu replied.

Gangu's father was not convinced but still permitted her to go with a long list of do's and don't.

The brightest day on all sets and Gangu begins the trip enthusiastically. The trip started from Mysore covering different places Hyderabad, Sikandarbad, Mumbai, Aurangabad and Pune.

The first destination of the trip was Hyderabad. Popularly known as the "City of Pearl". Historically monument Charminar is the centre of attraction of the City. As soon as they reached their booking were at the Osmania University hostel for their stay. It was a boys' hostel. Before Gangu and her group of friends were not aware that the hostel was of boys. All the boys went crazy. Seeing a batch of girls they started cheering and giggling as if it was like a group of fairies landing at their place. Gangu and her friends were in great shock. They went for an outing to visit different places in Hyderabad. Gangu and her teammates were amazed by the historical monuments of Hyderabad and they enjoyed the trip.

One day while coming back from the trip to the hostel Gangu found something strange. Suddenly she saw a group of boys calling her name reptively Gangu! Gangu! Gangu! They were yelling at the top of the voice.

Gangu was astonished, puzzled and shocked.

How could they know my name? Gaugu told to herself.

Along with her the other girl and professors were in shock. Wondering what is happening?

Unbelievable shock all went to their rooms. Professors were all scared. They rested in the hostel room. This incident was unforgettable and another incident took place in the span of a few time. The bright lightening of the rooms turned into dark and it was powered off. As the room turned dark all the girls got frightened and they moved out of the room into the corridor. Just wondering what was happening and trying to reach the professor girls came out. Again group of boys came around the Gangu by circling her up. They were trying to even hold her hand. She was fortunate enough that she managed to escape from there. That was a haunted memory that scared her professors and other friends. Her friend was repeatedly saying, "We will not say anything about what has happened here." And they did so no one knew what had happened on the trip to Hyderabad.

Then they moved to the next destination which was Sikandrabad. Coming from a bad experience in Hyderabad, the Sikandrabad trip was a booster. One of the reminiscences which Gangu held was the melodies singing competition. It was the full moon night, the beauty of the moon was on the peak and the stage was all set to get lost in the euphony.

Like always singing and dancing is a passion of Gangu. Gangu was a trained dancer of Kathak and Bharatanatyam. She has won many prestigious awards for dancing. She was most delighted about the singing competition. A bright smile like a moon was on her face and her eyes sparkling with joy. Lights were turned off in order not to recognise who was singing. The competition began with rhymes and the melody was at its peak. Fireflies illuminate the darkness. Now it was Gangu's turn to perform. Gangu was energetic and excited to perform.

Gangu went on the spotlight ready to rock. Mellifluous and sweet voice captured the heart of the audience. As it was all dark it was difficult to recognise who was singing. The audience went crazy to know who was singing and the stage was all on fire. The audience was deeply touched by the rhyme. They were lost in the dreamland assuming the fairy was singing. They couldn't stop themselves, they tried their best to recognise who was singing.

The song which Gangu chose to sing is Aa Neela Gagan Tale Pyar hum Karen. The audience was cheering with joy. They started illuminating the place with a torch to recognise who was singing. But they couldn't find who was singing as it was deep dark all around. It was only a melodious voice all in the air. It is a mystery of that euphonious up till now.

The journey was complete and they came back to Mercara. The trip package of trailers, adventures, horror and mystery. After coming back from the trip nobody could utter a word of what had happened on the trip. Gangu too has kept this secret buried through decades.

Academics was not her piece of cake. She was an average IQ student in academics. She would love to take responsibility and coordinate with different departments. She has served in different departments in the college. She was the fine arts secretary of the college. There was a boom in the entertainment industry of our country. It was the beginning of the film industry. The craze of film stars was at the pinnacle. Gangu coordinated with the team to call a superstar of the 90s Dilip Kumar. She came to know from somewhere that Dilip Kumar was at Mercara for a shoot. So they manage to invite him to a college fest. Gangu was so excited but went with the flow as she managed to be part of it.

As soon as Gangu's father came to know about this he was annoyed.

He ordered Gangu not to go to this event.

As rebellious as always Gangu refuses to accept the order of her father.

I have coordinated this event. I can't take a bad step, she said to her father.

Gangu's father, exasperated, didn't utter a word.

As the elders of that time used to think, being a film star is not a respectable profession. For them, it would not make any difference to meeting a film star.

The fact was that Gangu's parents were extra protective towards her.

"Her friends used to always say to her, you are like a parrot kept in a golden cage. If it comes out, the crow will catch it".

Finally, Gangu went to the college and coordinated all with the the utmost spirit. The college was decorated aesthetically. Gangu was not that excited but she was happy. A storm of students started gathering. The Golden period has finally arrived, meeting the famous superstar of Bollywood, Dilip Kumar. A glance at the star watch is different to get. But for Gangu it was all easy as she was coordinating for the event.

Gangu narrated, that Dilip Kumar looks much more handsome in real life than on screen.

Overall the event went smoothly and it was a delightful experience for everyone. For many their biggest dream comes true! Gangu was blissed and at the top of the world. Gangu was God gifted with the managerial skills which she carried forward in various stages of her life. Gangu is a girl with dreams and wants to fly high.

# CHAPTER FOUR

# After Graduation Tales

There comes a shakable time in a woman's life. Gangu completed her graduation and was delighted. Gangu was ambitious and she wanted to spread her wings. Many of her relatives suggested her father let her do a job and build her career. Unfortunately, her father was not in favour; he believed the neediest people should be allowed to work rather than rich ones. It was the early days of Indian independence, and India was growing rapidly. The new job openings were all over. Likewise, one search job opening drew the attention of Gangu. It was the opening for the cabin crew of Air India owned by the government. As Gangu was an explorer she was most fascinated about this opening.

She also says this quite often, Madikeri is a lovely place but for me, I found that it is limited. I wanted to explore and see the world. As soon as she saw this advertisement in the newspaper she contacted the given number. Her qualifications matched the opening and they assessed her for the further process of selection, that is the interview which was in Bombay known as Mumbai today. Getting permission from the father to go for an interview was like walking on thin ice.

Before going to her father for permission Gangu spoke with her mother. Her mother was convinced and carried word forward to her father. As usual, her father was not in her favour and she dropped out. They try to connect for an interview several times at last Gangu refuses them saying she is not interested. That's how Gangu gave up a golden opportunity to explore the world.

Gangu needed to stay at home after graduating. Training to make an idle wife was on fire. Gangu being Gangu refuses to do cooking. She is aloof towards cooking. Her mother would ask to cook while her father would protect her. She is a child. She will learn over time. Gangu would dance in joy. Mother being mother sent Gangu to her aunt's place to learn cooking. As Gangu didn't have a one per cent interest in cooking, the first task assisted was to make chapati. It was annoying for her as the maid was instructing her to make perfect chapati on the first attempt. Gangu blew a fuse, threw the chapati and went off. That was the end of cooking chapter after that Gangu never went into the kitchen in life.

# CHAPTER FIVE

# Marriage—Beginning of Doomsday

Early marriages were generally regarded favourably in Indian society, which placed a great cultural focus on marriage and family. People were frequently infatuated with the concept of marriage, and elaborate, lavish weddings, known as "Big Indian fat weddings," were famous across the world for their grandeur and festivities. Late teens and early twenties were thought to be the best ages for marriage since they were mature enough to take on parental duties and have a family. This cultural norm endured for centuries, impacting societal expectations and altering the life paths of many young individuals. Gangu was to be in her early twenties. As Gangu completed her graduation she was flooded with proposals. To be honest, Gangu was not interested in marriage.

In the beginning, she would reject the proposal by commenting, this boy is fat!

I don't like his looks! He looks too arrogant blah blah blah!

At last, Gangu stopped commenting and told her parents to select a partner for her. Giving crucial responsibility to her parents she was at peace. Her parents always loved her. She was the most pampered one. Gangu was sure that her parents would find someone compatible, the best man in the universe.

Destiny was preparing something harsh, the beginning of doom days. Gangu was not someone who would go against her father's command; she was an ideal daughter of her parents. It turns all silent before the storm hits the shore. The search for Gangu 's spouse was on. The fascinating proposal came to Gangu's father. A charming man located in Aden, Yamen. Before that, they used to reside in Somaliland. Due to the atrocity of war, they came to Madikeri. The boy's father was an O.B.E and had a very admiring personality. He had a good command of the language he would speak with a British accent.

Gangu has never seen them before but they were part of their community. The boy's aunt was staying in Madikeri through her the proposal came to her father. She describes the boy as a prince of a fairy tale.

Narrating all false. My sister's son is a perfect match. She told Gangu's father. Additionally, the family is well-settled abroad. She said all lies.

That's how she attracted the Gangu's father toward the proposal.

She also told the boy is doing a Bachelor of Commerce from Oxford University.

Sounds great, doesn't it? Knowing everything still knowing nothing. Gangu's father agreed to the proposal and has given consent too. The news of Gangu's proposal spread like a fire to the community.

Each one of them came to Gangu's father and suggested to him not to get her married to him. One of close relatives said these people do not match our status.

Gangu's professors too came to Gangu's father and told him not to get her marry to him, she was such a good girl. She deserves someone better!

One of the cousin sisters of Gangu's father was constantly advising him.

She said, they are not good people, they are very greedy. Don't let her marry him.

The whole community was trying to convince the father to not let this marriage happen. It was like when consent is given it can't be taken back.

Even the hospital staff of Gangu's father was requesting him not to marry her to him.

But the Gangu's father did not pay attention to anyone and did what he wanted to do. Poor mother of Gangu's was watching this all happening but can't help it out. Being an ideal daughter Gangu didn't utter a word. She just thought it was written in her destiny.

Before marrying him Gangu hadn't met them before or even seen them. But luckily once she went to her cousin's wedding there she saw the mother of him for the first time. The bright face of Gangu got pale. She was not at all happy after seeing her. She has no personality and is not ever a status match. What would a broken girl do? She just kept quiet. For the engagement, they bought a cheap diamond ring for Gangu. But it could not impress Gangu the diamond was so dull that Gangu felt like throwing it due to the bowl of patience she drank having control.

During the cousin's marriage, Gangu's brother saw her for the first time.

The first word that he utters after seeing is, you're marrying a servant son Gangu!

Refuse! He is not a good match.

Helpless Gangu's brother told her till the day of marriage to refuse but she didn't.

What Father has told, us will happen! Gangu has a strong belief in it.

Nothing would hardly make a difference if she refused also.

No one was happy with the marriage ceremony which was about to happen. In fact from the day the proposal came, nobody was delighted. Gangu just accepted what was happening and moved on. Preparations were on for the big day. Around 3000 guests were invited to the wedding. It was all grand as Subbaya was a reputed name in the community.

Dooms Day ( Marriage)

# CHAPTER SIX

# Day of Marriage

It was a big day in Gangu's life, unaware of what could happen in future. The mesmerizing beauty of Gangu was breathtaking. There is a package of emotion carried to a girl being a bride. It is anxious, delighted, nervous and so on. Unlike all the other girls Gangu was not that excited and happy for a marriage. But she knows to hide them with a broad smile. She wore an elegant saree embracing golden Polka dots for the wedding ceremony. Royal gold jewelry and most importantly Indian wedding garland. They have weddings separately. Her partner has a marriage in Mysore while Gangu has her marriage in Madikeri. Guests also visit separately. The wedding is followed by Muhurat and then by lunch. In the evening the groom comes to the bride's place and they have some ceremony and rituals together.

While doing the rituals the Gangu found him least interested and just doing everything like a robot. The seed of sorrow in Gangu's life begins on the day of the wedding only. He was rude, detached and self-centred and did not care about anyone. Overall the ceremony Gangu was in grief but she made it with a fake smile.

Hidden and untold Gangu went on for a new journey. Right on the first day of the wedding, she was welcomed with thorns. It was the ritual that a new bride should carry a torso of gifts. Like the ritual, Gangu also brought. The next day of the wedding the box was opened by in-laws.

Gangu was the only daughter and the most loved one. The things which Gnagu brought with her were giant; it took more than two people to lift them The box consisted of seventy-plus premium sarees, exclusive jewellery and other stuff such as purses, footwear and so on. Gangu's sister-in-law and mother-in-law took it out. The neighbours and other community people were called to see the stuff which Gangu brought. The sister-in-law ruins the event by shouting and creating unnecessary disputes.

Her sister-in-law started to taunt Gangu's mother-in-law by saying cruelly,

You have brought a rich daughter-in-law.

At our time you didn't give us anything like that.

She was jealous of Gangu. She even stole her things.

As usual, Gangu was watching the dispute quietly.

Her sister-in-law was the most cruel one on her in-laws' side. While the other sister-in-law was a gem, sweet and kind. She was like a friend to her. Coming to Mother-in-law was a kind lady who always supported her. She always calls her a 'child' and she has an affection towards her. Her Father-in-law was a sharp and smart man. Gangu's Brother-in-law was neutral in his world. Soon after the wedding, the true faces of her in-laws were before her. Gangu's patience journey begins.

Soon after that incident, Gangu went to her mother's place. Her mother was delighted to see her.

Mixed emotions Gangu's mother raised a question to Gangu. How are you?

Gangu replied, Forget that you'll have done my wedding assume that it was my eleventh day ceremony.

With tears in her eyes, Gangu added, don't ask me anything now.

And she went to the in-laws house.

Marriage is the journey of two souls hence the partner should be chosen wisely. Unlike Gangu's situation where hold world was standing with her but her father just refused. Once Gangu's mother-in-law told Gangu's father before marriage.

Don't marry your lovely daughter to my son he is not good.

Imagine a mother remarking about her son but still it could not make any difference to Gangu's father.

Gangu just heard her father saying, She is a madwoman.

Anyway, Gangu just thought it was part of destiny. What has to happen will happen. At her father's will Gangu got married to him.

Life after the wedding was no peace for Gangu. Her husband had no affection towards her; he was in his world. Soon after a few days of marriage, Gangu's father-in-law sponsored a trip to Singapore on the cruise. The shore of the cruise was located in Bombay. From Madikeri to Bombay they went by train. Gangu had taken the money for tickets for the train from her father. It was an embarrassing situation for Gangu after reaching the station her husband did not have money to get tickets. Gangu had a little money with her and she handed it over to him and then they boarded the train. He was not responsible. That's how their trip began.

It was a huge luxurious cruise. The cruise consisted of a movie theatre, activity area, banquet, swimming pool, dining hall and many shopping centres. As soon as they entered the cruise he just vanished somewhere. There was no joy in the trip, it was all loneliness with Gangu. While onboarding on the cruise. Gangu had made some of the best friends. There is one of the Pakistani family. The man was an Income Tax Commissioner and her wife was a doctor and they had three children along with them. It was so noticeable that everyone was saying, where is your husband, we don't see him much with you. Gangu would spend hours with them on the cruise.

There was also another father-daughter on the cruise. They were very friendly with her. The father was an assistant commissioner of police in Singapore. They were getting back to Singapore after the trip. They were kind and caring. There was a group which was also onboard on a cruise. They asked Gangu not to mix with them because they were not good people. They were smuggling from Bombay to Singapore.

Keep them hello only. They even gave her the contact number and invited her along with her husband for dinner in Singapore.

It was the first international visit of Gangu to Singapore. Gangu was amazed to explore Singapore. After reaching there nothing was booked. Gangu has a little currency exchange that he also took away from her. He was not able to find a place to stay so contented the brother-in-law's friends. They were so good that they called her into their home. But Gangu felt very bad as they gave their bedroom to them. She got angry as her father had never stayed in anybody's house but he would always book a hotel room.

With boiling anger Gangu commanded him, get me to a hotel room whether it is cheap but I won't stay here or she will stay on the road

That's the surprise she had throughout the trip. Well, the rest of the time her husband was out somewhere.

While travelling on a ship to Singapore she got an invitation for lunch from an Assistant Commissioner of Police. They were her new friends. As they gave her their contact number she connected and got the location. Gangu and husband went for a lunch. Gangu was astonished after seeing the location. It was a huge bungalow surrounded all over greener. The ambience inside the bungalow was great and well-maintained. Gangu had a great time with never-ending conversations. The food was delicious and memorable.

The daughter was sweet handling all arrangements by herself while the father went out for a minute to attend urgent call.

As soon as he went Gangu's husband said, Let's stay here today.

It was a wonderful place. Annoyed, Gangu replied, Just have lunch and move out.

At the time of leaving they handed a gift as a sweet gesture to Gangu. They were in contact for many years but due to pressure in life she lost it.

Throughout the journey, he had hardly spent any time with Gangu. No great memories she could recall with him. They have just seen three movies together. The rest of the time where he was Gangu was not aware. That's how they return from the trip back to Bombay.

After returning from the trip landed at her sister-in-law's place. She was the most cruel lady Gangu had ever met. She has opened the suitcase which Gangu has bought for herself without her knowledge. Sister-in-law would instruct her to wear her old saree and she would wear Gangu's new saree. That was the first and last time Gangu stayed at her place. Gangu's sister-in-law made her life miserable.

# CHAPTER SEVEN

# Migrated to Aden

The new journey begins in Gangu's life. New challengers were waiting for her. Unknown of what would be the future Gangu boarded on ship. Bombay to Aden was a four-day journey. As usual, as they are on board the ship he has just vanished. Gangu was mentally prepared for it and she managed it all. The ship was crowded by Gujarati's and Parsi's. Many Gujaratis thought that Gangu was a dancer and gave her their contact number. They told Gangu, we would send our children to learn dancing from you. Gangu took the contact number and kept quiet.

The ship reached the port of Aden. It was a different place for Gangu coming from a small town. The ship was coming all over from Australia and going to England. On the same ship, there was the father-in-law's friend and his wife. Father-in-law and brother-in-law came to the port to meet them. Gangu was not aware of this couple until they met them at the port. They were having only one day as the ship was at the port then sailing off to England. Father-in-law and brother-in-law brought their car along with them. They took them for lunch at a pleasant restaurant and had delicious food there. Soon after that, they took them shopping. Gangu and her husband were along with them. Gangu was astounded after seeing the shops. Aden is a shopper's paradise. It was duty-free. After that father-in-law and brother-in-law went to see off them.

Gangu went to her new house where she lived for a few years. It was a pleasant bungalow that was given to her father-in-law by the British government. He was working with the British government on the contract. While both the sons were staying with him. They were doing government services. On the first day of a new country, Gangu didn't have great memories. Her husband came to change his clothes in the room and went. The existence of Gangu hardly made a difference in his life. The father-in-law took leave on that day and the brother-in-law went for work.

Gangu was alone in her bedroom. They used to get a lunchbox from outside that saved Gangu from cooking. The brother-in-law came back from work. Along with her father-in-law and brother-in-law, Gangu had her first dinner in Aden. Soon after the dinner both of them went to sleep.

Innocent Gangu remained awake, impatiently awaiting his return. She had no idea where he was or when he'd return, but her anxiety kept her awake. The hours passed slowly, and he didn't get home until , around 2 a.m.

In real concern, Gangu said, "Where did you go? "Why is it so late?" Her tone was laced with anxiety and fear.

However, when the harsh guy heard her questioning him, he became enraged. Without hesitation, he lifted his hand and slapped Gangu on the face.

The agony of the slap was both physical and emotional, leaving Gangu upset and perplexed by his strong response.

Gangu was shocked after receiving the slap. She felt extremely vulnerable and frightened. He didn't stop there. He roared at her, "How dare you ask me!"

He began flinging obscenities and foul language at her, screaming at the top of his voice.

That can't be printed in the book.

Gangu never dared to question him again for the rest of their time together till he left in 1985 after that horrible occurrence. This was the start of a sad chapter in her life, the first day in Aden. Gangu quietly accepted his brutality from that day on, swallowing her pride and sipping the bitter drop of patience regularly. Fear and agony became daily companions, yet she persevered with a quiet resilience that marked her strength.

*The shining moon faded away,*
*Darkest surrounded all around,*
*What turns a life has taken all the sorrow around,*
*With the hope for better life sunsets,*
*My heart is waiting to see bright sunshine again.*

Gangu had never imagined the horror her life would become after marriage; it was the worst calamity she had ever experienced. Every day brought fresh difficulties and painful memories, as all of the promises made to her proved untrue. Every day, Gangu found herself sipping from the cup of patience, bearing the harshness of the man she had married, who appeared more like a beast than a spouse. He would beat her viciously with a hockey stick, leaving behind blistering scars that she would hide under her saree every day. The physical misery was only equalled by the emotional and psychological wounds she carried, as she lived in terror and silence, unwilling to share her pain with anybody.

Father-in-law and brother-in-law knew what was happening still they never opened their mouths.

*A Girl lost her smile,*
*Who cares about happiness,*
*Who stands for sorrow,*
*All good turns to bad the mental peace is gone!*
*Die each day still seems to look like everything is perfect,*
*That's life when a girl is married to the wrong man.*

# CHAPTER EIGHT

# Journey of Working

Soon after a few days after being in Aden, Gangu started working. The evil man would provide nothing but for sure hit her badly for money. Managing the financial turbulence Gangu joined the Aden Treasury before joining the work in the year 1964 May. Gangu had an abortion in February 1964. Her father-in-law was in tears as if the world would end. Later on, Gangu joined the work in the same year. The job was nearby for the house. Luckily all of them had individual cars Gangu too was arranged for a car.

She joined as a temporary hand where she would work from 8 AM to 12:30 PM while the other would work from 7:30 AM to 3 PM. The Aden Treasury was full of a workforce of Indians–Gujarati, Parsi and locals that are Arabs and English people. At that time federation was in the hands of Britishers.

Her boss was a kind and wise man. Right at the time of the interview, He gave her a piece of fantastic advice, look girl! keep your ears and eyes open and keep your mouth shut you will learn a lot.

Gangu preserved the piece of advice in her treasure and carried it all through her life.

Unaware of the work environment doing the job was the most crucial responsibility on Gangu's shoulders. Their In-laws were greedy for money and therefore they did the wedding. Gangu stopped asking for money instant started working and providing them. Anyway her journey begins, she knows nothing. Even her father-in-law said, Your husband has taken a lot of money. You should work and pay back. Even to buy a slice of bread they would ask her to buy. Well, rude to what extent?

On the first day of office, she didn't know how to pick up the telephone in hand. Suddenly the telephone started ringing loudly. Gangu is scared and tries to pick up the call. She just picks up the telephone in the wrong direction. It was all over humour at the office everyone was laughing at her.

That's how she began. She left one hour early on the first day assuming the job timing was till 11:30 AM which was till 12:30. Thanks to God! Nobody questioned her the next day even her boss.

Gangu then began to work seriously, even though her hand had been gravely hurt as a result of her husband's aggression. She'd conceal the injuries behind her saree pallu. Despite the challenges, she found her job engaging and learnt rapidly. Gangu has strong grasping abilities, allowing her to quickly learn new talents.

Once Gangu out of respect called her boss 'sir' But the boss found it to be strange.

He told Gangu, there is no one sir.

Just call me by my name.

Gangu captured it into her mind and never called sir after his advice.

Her immediate boss was Gujarati and proved to be an excellent mentor. He encouraged her to study by teaching her how to keep record books and raise funds. His advice was valuable in her career progress. With his assistance, Gangu began to thrive in her profession, eventually gaining confidence and independence. Despite the difficulties she encountered at home, her employment provided her with a sense of purpose and a route to rebuilding her life.

Everyone was kind and supportive making a friendly atmosphere to learn and adjust. They even allowed her to go from department to department and learn. Over time they found Gangu to be dedicated and having marvellous grasping power. They promoted her to the Civil Services Housing Loan Scheme in-charge. Her job was to call for funds and grant loans to eligible local civil servants. Gangu was enthusiastic especially to make a balance sheet since it was different from her educational background.

Due to the Civil Services Houseing Scheme, she had made great connections. Some of them are the Chief Ministry Secretary, Attorney General Commissioner Aden, Police Commissioner, Income tax Commissioner, Migration Commissioner and Customs Commissioner used to walk into her office quite often. It was a wonderful feeling for Gangu they would straight come to her office to work. When she would go by car on the road the police would just salute her at the traffic light. It was the best phase for her. She was rocked to new highs while at home struggles remained the same. The day she would get the salary he would take it away. She would hide the money to run the house. He would hit her cruelly. He had made her life miserable for money.

Meanwhile mother-in-law landed in Aden then the entire pattern changed of home. She would manage the house chores. She would be upset when he would not come home. She once told Gangu, let's stand together at the door and we will hit him together. She also told Gangu many times that we have ruined your life. Her mother-in-law was a good lady and had affection towards her. She treats her like her own daughter. That's how days passed Gangu's life became hell. Her patience was tested to the highest level.

Right from the first day as she joined the work at Aden Treasury Gangu was waiting for the day to get her salary. It was her new experience earning money from her sweat. She even thought of buying a saree to make it memorable. Gangu was at the top of the hill and she achieved her first salary. Her hands were shaking and her eyes were brightening with joy. As soon as she reached home her joy turned into sorrow. Gangu's husband snatched all the money and didn't leave a penny with her. All the dreams turn into nightmares. The helpless Gangu wouldn't do anything and kept patience.

He started getting more aggressive towards her. If she could not give the money he would beat, bash, and kick her with spike cicket boots all the energy. A man with no heart.

She almost left hope for life. There was no joy in her life. The whole world was a dark place for her. She had stopped loving her life. She was so frustrated that she

wanted to end her life. She tried to commit suicide but the will of God was something different he saved her. Somewhere her father-in-law was aware of her mental state. Father-in-law asked brother-in-law to remove all poisonous things from the home. Later on, Gangu realized that she was wrong. Ending life is not the solution. She kept hoping for a better tomorrow and carrying on. Time is the best healer.

# CHAPTER NINE

# Mischief of In-Law

Gangu wanted to open a bank account to have some savings. It was easy for her to open an account as she had good networking. Unrealizing the fact Gangu told her father-in-law, I am opening a bank account. Her father-in-law was the most clever one. He suggested, Open a joint bank account. Just creating a new way to let his son enjoy more. Undoubtedly Gangu was the most obedient one. She opened a joint bank account keeping respect to the advice of the elder. Gangu also opened an individual bank account.

She was unaware of the mischief that they were plotting against her. Suddenly one day she went to the bank to check her account balance. Gangu went into great shock that there was not a penny in the account. Gangu tried to connect with bank staff and consult the issue. She found one of the staff member was involved with her husband as soon as she came to know she rushed towards that man whose she found the culprit.

On reaching there Gangu asked, how can you give the money without my knowledge?

It's a single account of Gangu. I am going to the bank manager and complaining Gangu told the man.

He started begging by joining his hands. They'll remove me from the job please don't go. I have to take care of the family, please! Don't go to them. Gangu being the emotional person forgives him. And told don't repeat this. A girl with a golden heart! Her husband and bank employee would have gone to jail. On the same evening, Gangu's husband bashed her badly with foul language that can't be printed in the book.

# CHAPTER TEN

# Beginning of Motherhood—
# Elder Son's Arrival

Gangu's life was filled with instability, yet she confronted it bravely, always managing to grin through the trials. Her daily trip from job to home, along with the atrocities perpetrated by her spouse, became an unending part of her routine. Despite the difficulties, she faced life with courage and elegance. To her, life was like a rose banquet—beautiful but thorny. Gangu persisted, drawing strength from her inner fortitude and the steadfast support of those who cared for her. Throughout it all, she maintained optimism, hoping that brighter days would inevitably arrive.

Gangu got her hope for life, that is, she was expecting a child. Gangu was delighted, hoping the coming child would be the reason to live a better life. As Gangu knew she was expecting she started saving for delivery and post-delivery care. While father-in-law would not give a penny whole arranging of bread and butter responsibility was a burden on the shoulders of Gangu. Father-in-law and brother-in-law knew what was happening still they never opened the mouths. Hiding for the guilty man who has no sense of responsibility. His atrocities do not stop here looking at his wife's condition he becomes the wildest.. He started beating her more intensively a cruel and wicked man. Gangu would feel extreme pain when he hit her on the lower back as he came to know that he started hitting her on her lower back. Money! Money! Money! was the only word he would have in his dirty mouth.

Meanwhile with all the pain Gangu somehow managed. Gangu would go to the office with a huge baby bump. As Gangu was a temporary employee she had maternity leave only for thirty days. Gangu discussed taking maternity leave after child delivery into this world. Couragely she fought with all the odds to get her child into the world. Hiding the scars and being wounded was the new normal for her. Whatever was going on at her home she never disclosed to anyone. She never shares with her parents and dearest one. Gangu always stayed firm and dealt with her battles by herself.

During the year 1964, Aden was struggling for independence. Strikes and bloodshed were all around. Gangu has watched all of these incidents during her pregnancy. Every day on the way to the office one or another was killed in front of her police, the commissioner and so on. Sometimes it was so terrifying because of the bombing people were killed into pieces. Bloody streets everywhere killing. Gangu was scared but she had no choice. One day before her child was born her husband again started demanding money. Again he beat her harshly during the third trimester of pregnancy. He had no mercy for her. She was just like an ATM for him. The baby was born on 12 July 1965 where else her husband kicked her on her back badly on 8 July for money.

It hit her so badly that her face became pale from pain. The next day she started getting labor pain slowly and gradually the intensity of pain increased. Gangu was rushed to the hospital. On 12 July 1965 Gangu gave birth to an adorable boy child. Gangu was most delighted after seeing her son. She named him Vikram. The feeling of being a mother can't be narrated in words. While looking at her child Gangu's eyes brighten up with tears of joy. She was admiring the whole world in him. Vikram was a wonderful child. He was fair, chubby and cute. His lovely face illuminates light with round eyes.

Suddenly a huge explosion took place in the hospital. People were runing helter-skelter. Everywhere was unrest. After two moments of joy, Gangu went into shock thinking about what to do. Gangu with a shaking hand took the baby into her hand and sat at the bed. Gangu was weak as she delivered a baby a few hours before the explosion therefore running was not possible for her. Anyway with all of the courage sat there holding the baby tightly. They manage to survive a horrifying bomb explosion.

As the situation became cool Gangu wanted to get back to the home. As she knew Aden's condition. Deep in her heart, she was thinking it would be the last day of her life. As the hospital's outside condition became better she wanted to leave the hospital but hospital staff just stopped her from going due to a pending bill payment. Suddenly Gangu recall she had given her money before going to the labour room to her husband. She also told him not to spend this money since need it for delivery.

At that time he just nodded his head.

Gangu asked him, give me that money.

Carelessly he replied, I don't have any money!

Gangu was somewhere aware that he would do such a thing.

She requested the hospital staff to let her go. She will get back home and bring the money.

Luckily they were kind Gangu went to the house. As soon as Gangu reached home she took all the boxes of her jewellery where she secretly hide money. After that, she again went to the hospital and paid all the bills.

Vikram was one of the most loved the child. Gangu was on maternity leave for thirty days after that her neighbours and friends helped her to get a nanny. There were some Indian ladies but they were not taking care of the baby. Anyway, Gangu had to leave for her work with a heavy heart so she was searching for someone responsible. Gangu had no choice but to leave his lovely child back at home and get back to work for money. She can't expect financial help from her father-in-law and brother-in-law and her husband is least bothered by his responsibility.

Finally, Gangu found a Somali lady to take care of her child. She was a tall Arab lady. She had an affection for Vikram. She would say, Habibi! Habibi! habibi! to Gangu's child. Gangu kept her from 8 AM to 2 PM as their salaries were too high and with limited money Gangu had to manage all.

Vikram was most loved by everybody. A child that brings joy. Opposite her house, there was a centre. The principal of that centre was most fond of Vikram.

Each time when she held the baby she would say, My Million Dollar Baby!

The condition of Aden was getting worse now and then there was a strike, bombing, killing and no peace.

Gangu and other Government employees were getting notice again and again to be on the job. Which clearly says that if not onboard to work straight away will be terminated.

The principal of the centre was aware of the Gangu situation.

She told Gangu I know how much you need this job.

You go to work, I will take care of your baby.

Due to a general strike, the Nanny was not able to come hence the principal would take him to her cabin. Gangu would early morning prepare all the necessary things required for the day for her child. She had even given her the times when to feed the baby.

The principal was a kind lady and helped Gangu a lot. Throughout the day she not only took care of the child but also gave regular updates of what the baby was doing.

She would send her small messages,

Gangu baby is playing!

Gangu baby is sleeping!

Gangu baby is eating!

For that, Gangu would have notes of what her child is doing.

After baby Gangu got her determination for life. Raising him and growing together. Meanwhile, his husband turned for the worse day by day. Once he had beaten Gangu with a cricket bet which fractured her foot. The only demand that he has is money. Gangu was not aware of the activities which he did with money. Nor Gangu has even asked him. The slap which he had hit her on the first day of Aden was unforgettable for Gangu.

*Unshattered journey of horror,*
*Life has taught me another corner,*
*Whom to say what in heart,*
*Are you in someone's heart?*
*Do not cover the curtain, the wounds you wear,*
*Let them cure by themselves.*

Meanwhile, there was a currency change in Aden. Before they were using East African Shilling now shifting towards Dinaars. Looking at Gangu's past performance and dedication towards work they have signed her to do this work as well. There was an Indian who was already part of the currency exchange.

Instead of asking senior, they asked Gangu to do currency change work. The senior became annoyed and started making derogatory remarks.

He said, just because she is beautiful you are keeping her at every place.

From the beginning, Gangu doesn't want to be part of this work due to her baby's duties. Gangu's boss requested her to do so. Gangu told her boss to give this work to him only. He has been doing this work for a long time.

Gangu's Boss didn't listen to her and made an offer.

He told Gangu, she would be paid per file.

That's how nobody would be at a loss, he added.

Gangu agreed at last.

After getting the responsibility of currency change Gangu would carry the files along with her at home. She would take care of her child as well as she would do the office work. One day she was sitting on the balcony doing work his son was playing on the

floor. While moving from there one of her neighbors saw that. He just sent her daughter to Gangu and asked her to give us to take care of your child while she was doing work. That's how the entire world was opening arms standing for her to help.

**Vikram–6 months–Aden**

While Gangu was most popularly known as Wahida Rahama. Gangu has an appearance similar to Wahida Rahama's while matching Wahida Rahama and Gangu's photos people couldn't find any difference in both. Gangu was a Xerox copy of Wahida Rahama's form face structure to appearance. Whenever Gangu would go to the theatre to watch movies, people would think that she was Wahida Rahama sitting there and the crowd would go crazy.

This doesn't happen to Gangu once but it happened with her multiple times. At last, whenever Gangu used to go for a movie she would come out 10 to 20 minutes before watching the climax of the movie. She was treated as if she were a celebrity. She was also popularly called Wahida Rahman in Aden Treasury. Meanwhile, Gangu never took advantage of this and she would hide her face wherever she felt she needed to.

Gangu was experiencing something fresh in Aden. Some elements of her profession were positive, providing her with new abilities and prospects for advancement, but others were intimidating and filled with uncertainty. Gangu experienced a range of emotions as he adjusted to life in a new location, distant from home. She had obstacles that challenged her fortitude and perseverance, but she also had moments of joy and learning. Gangu worked her way through the uncertainty, embracing the new experiences with drive and hope for a brighter future.

# CHAPTER ELEVEN

# Trip to Europe

As Aden's condition was getting worse Gangu shifted to Seraa Island but before that, Gangu went for a trip to Europe. But before she had to shift the things from Crater, to Seraa island. Luckily, her brother-in-law told Gangu to go peacefully. He will manage all the things to get shifted before they come back. He also added land directly from airport to Seraa Island. Gangu was happy as she was stressed about how to manage the shift. Packing things and then getting loaded into the vehicle all stress just went off.

Her brother-in-law was a supportive and caring figure in Gangu's life. He had a strong attachment to her son, Vikram, which provided solace to Gangu in the middle of her difficulties. Despite the hardships she encountered, Gangu continued on another voyage to an unknown location. This was her first overseas journey with her son, Vikram. It was a huge milestone for Gangu, full of excitement and mixed feelings. She tackled the adventure with eagerness and dedication, eager to discover new vistas and have memorable experiences with her darling kid by her side.

Time flies so steadily. It was yesterday when Vikram was born. Now it's time to celebrate his first birthday. Gangu was most delighted by her apple of eye growing. The only motivation to live life was all because of her child. They had his first birthday on a ship named "Marconi" They had a huge grand party on the ship. The crowd was all cheering and enjoying the celebration. Gangu dresses up Vikram for celebration with affection. Lovely Vikram at his mother's arm throughout the event. The time came for Vikram with his little hands along with his mother holding the knife to cut cake. Gangu with sparkling eyes hiding her tears of joy cut the cake. The event was followed by dinner with melodious music.

The ship sailed through the Suez Canal via Egypt then the ship reached Italy, Naples. During the trip, Gangu ends up making two new friends. They were Arab men in their 40's. While sailing in the ship Gangu made unforgettable memories with her child– the first birthday of her adorable child.

As soon as they landed in Italy they started their European tour by road. Europe was cheering with joy. All through the Europe trip, Gangu wore sarees as she walked on the street. It would make people crazy. Pretty young Gangu would feel delighted for unbeatable attention. Looking at her people would hug her as the saree was a new thing for them. They would say her "belleza".Her husband was along with her wherever she went and ended the day with a fight.

Overall the trip was fantastic Italy welcomed them with an open arm. In the evening whenever Gangu wants to go for an outing the maid of the hotel would say to her don't worry I will look after your child. Like that, the people of Italy were kind and helpful. Of course, the trip doesn't end here Gangu is someone who goes beyond imagination to explore the destination. Luckily, on every trip, she ends up making wonderful friends.

Gangu was cooking something adventurous. You wanted to explore Rome by night. Her husband was least bothered by whatever she was doing. One thing is that he would stay with her and baby on the trip throughout the day but in the evening he is to fly away somewhere. Anyways Gangu manages to explore Rome in the evening. She contacted the new friends she had made on the ship. They were shipping magnets. Both of them helped and pampered her a lot.

Gangu requested one of them that I wanted to see the Roma at night.

They instructed her, "What will you see at night? It's not good. It is not for you.

But Gangu kept on insisting, please want to see! Gangu did her head to toe to explore Rome at night.

Finally, they agreed with her and Gangu went to see the Roma along with them.

As soon as Gangu went out to see Rome at night it was horrible. What she had seen she wanted to get back to the hotel.

One of them told Gangu that I had given the clue before only.

You are a young girl, it's not for you. People were lost in another world doing awful activities on the streets of Rome.

Apart from this memory, Gangu has wonderful memories of Italy. Gangu visited today's attraction points of Italy, the Leaning Tower of Pisa. The icing on the cake was that they were allowed to get inside that Leaning Tower. Of course, it was dark from inside but as they reached the peak of the tower it was a joyful experience to see the city from the top. Gangu carrying her baby went straight to the peak of the tower adding everlasting memories of travel.

During the Europe trip, Gangu also visited Germany and Cologne. Cherishing country with lovely people who were heartwarming in nature. Gangu is a traveller by heart and couldn't miss an opportunity to explore. She visited a famous perfume factory called 4711 Eaude Cologne. The Factory was huge and had a unique way of working. The music is turned on while working.

Gangu as usual groomed well with a saree. There was a guide throughout the factory visit giving information about departments. As Gangu went her beauty captured everyone's attention. Gangu just thought they might be having a break.

As Gangu moves further the guide asks her to let's go back.

The guide also added the whole workforce is working. They just can't take their eyes looking at your beauty.

Innocent Gangu just smiled and her face turned red with shyness which made her move beautiful.

The Guide kept on saying, let's move otherwise they will make a huge loss.

As unique as always Gangu's beauty is mesmerizing. They were thrilled with saree.

She travelled to France however then she travelled from Holland to England.

After a joyful exploration of Italy, Gangu sailed from holland to England. After reaching England they went to London where her younger brother-in-law was studying. As a kind gesture her brother-in- law came to pick them up at the port. He was in tears after meeting her and delighted. It was his first meeting with Gangu as he was studying at an outstation and therefore couldn't attend the wedding. He started saying, this man doesn't deserve you. Why did you marry him? Even now it's not too late just go away. He has ruined your life. Anyways these were the common phrases Gangu used to heard some of her in-laws. Gangu can't back a step as her parents wouldn't support and they were the ones who pushed her into an unpeaceful situation.

*Gangu with elder son ( Vikram) in London*

On the other hand, her husband has no shame he would beat her in front of her brother-in-law. He did not have a pinch of respect and care for Gangu.

While the trip was going on she visited Bath and its neighboring place.

After reaching there her husband's violence went on to new heights. He would continuously fight with her and a greedy man of money snatched all the money. The survival of Gangu in London was becoming difficult; she had no penny with her. Then at last Gangu was left with no option but to call her brother-in-law for money. Gangu asks her brother-in-law to send some money to get back to Aden. She also gave a word that as soon as she reached back she would return the money.

Gangu got frustrated and annoyed and couldn't take the mischief of her husband in a strange country. As soon as she got the money Gangu booked the plane tickets and landed at Aden Island. While her husband was still in London. Gangu was unaware of what he was doing there. Gangu landed on Seraa Island and as soon as she reached there she gave back the money which she had borrowed from her brother-in-law. As her brother-in-law told her before the trip to Europe, he shifted all the things and arranged them properly at Seera Island's new house.

*With broken hearts destination change,*
*What are you waiting for heart says,*
*Those next destinations will teach what,*
*My heart is waiting for peace would the next destination will give.*
*Up the limitless sky would give me happiness that disappeared.*
*Oh! My creator I want a better day to live.*

# CHAPTER TWELVE

# Life in the Dark—Bombing All Around

Seera Island shone like a diamond in the blue ocean. Deserted mountains dominated the beach was a soft white powder, with pure waves lapping at the shore. There was a only narrow bridge on the island. The island is surrounded by fishers and a popular fishes seen are whales and kitefish.

As soon as Gangu landed she had to report for duty leaving an apple of the eye back at home. She missed him at the hours of her duty but she had no option but to leave him behind at home. The Somali Lady which she hired as a nanny for her child care came along with her at Seera Island.

While looking at her progress and dedication towards the work of Gaugu her manager and boss were impressed. They wanted to keep her permanent. They have done all the documentation and sent it to the higher authority to get permission to make her a permanent employee. While the higher authority didn't give her the green flag. They have a low mentality that she is young and beautiful therefore they are making her a permanent employee. Well, they do not even consider the contribution that she was making to Aden Treasury. Gangu on the other hand knew the fact as the struggle for independence went beyond the boundaries she would lose her job. Gangu doesn't have one per cent hope that they will make her a permanent employee. But for her son and carrying the household expenses she had to do a job.

If could get a better opportunity Gangu was in favour of quitting the existing job. But at the same time, she was too attached to the job as it was prestigious. Due to this job, Gangu has met people from all walks of life She even made connections and friends. The demand for money for her husband was increasing rapidly and even the child expenses were on her shoulders. Suddenly from somewhere Gangu heard that there was a vacancy for a teacher at a government college. Not giving a second thought Gangu just applied as soon as possible. She got a call for an interview. The head of the education department took her interview. Gangu got selected in the interview and onboarded to another job different from the previous one.

Meanwhile, her father-in-law gone back to India. He was working in the education department. As there were many vacancies before for teachers Gangu used to apply but didn't get a call for an interview. Luckily this time got the call for the interview.

Gangu went for an interview she was herself and was unaware that her father-in-law was working for the education department.

During the interview, the interviewer told her father-in-law's name.

Gangu was a puzzle as she had called her father-in-law's name.

The interviewer asked her do you know him?

Gangu said, yes of course! he is my father-in-law.

Then the interviewer asked her, do you know why you did not get a job before in teaching?

Gangu again got puzzled and said no nodding her head.

The interviewer disclosed, you know you don't get the job because of your father-in-law. He would not allow us to give you a job because he had a feeling that you would be in the higher grading than him.

As Gangu was a graduate they were given a higher position at that time. Gangu's father-in-law was just insecure about that.

Gangu does not comment on anything but her mind is flooding with many things. Even knowing the condition of Gangu and her husband nature father-in-laws have done. He was cruel and with poor mentality. Gangu was struggling for penny and penny of money due to her husband if she could have got the job earlier it would have helped her so much. But anyway Thank God! Father-in-law was not there in Aden she got the job.

Gangu was on the contract she was offered a good salary with all other benefits such as gratuity. Due to the wicked father and son, Gangu had struggled a lot. Anyways few people are in this world to make people's lives miserable and Gangu's father-in-law was one of them. It was a lengthy process before joining the college to teach.

Gangu said Goodbye to Aden Treasury. Treasury people were in sorrow, knowing Gangu was leaving the job. The application to make her a permanent employee was still pending. Anyway, Gangu predicted before that Aden would get independence and all of the employees would be thrown out of their jobs. Well, this was like saying goodbye to old and warm hearty welcome to new.

Everything started to settle and the wicked man came back to Aden from holidays in London to make the Gangu's life miserable again. Money! Money! Money! The only priority he has. He is just not bothered about how it is earned. He won't care even if you sell your organs and bring money for him, a man with no heart. Gangu was hoping that the salary increase would bring a better standard of living.

While the nanny she had hired was with them. She loved the baby the most. The violence of her husband was as usual nothing changed but he was scared of the nanny. The lady was tall and had a good physique. She adore Gangu and was always in her support. A woman with a golden heart. One day Gangu's husband was shouting cruelly in front of her. She wouldn't take it. Her face turned red in anger. She came to the room and said, Look here how dare you disrespect her and say a word to her. She is the one who gives me the salary. After that, he was so scared of her that he even did not open his mouth in front of her.

The nanny also added that everyone is saying, this man is not good. He asked his wife to work and take away the money. You're married but it seems that you have kidnapped her since the level of atrocities he did with his wife. The entire locality people were speaking like that about Gangu's husband. Gangu just kept on laughing and trying to calm her. Like that, she had mercy towards Gangu. Likewise, life was going on. They went to that extent that a sensible parent would never give their daughter to such a man.

Gangu would get some time to spend with her child. He was a good child. He didn't give her much stress and a happy child. The view outside the new house was dreamy. There was a sea which could be seen from her balcony. Cool and calm environment with breezy air. In the evening Gangu would go for a walk with her baby.

The seed of independence was getting deep roots. There was all-over bombing and bloodshed. Once Gangu was standing on the balcony of her apartment the Britishers came to know the terrorists were there in the mosque other side of bridge. They targeted it straight on the mosque to bombing the whole structure of the mosque just vanished in a few minutes. One could see the bodies falling from terrorists who were top of the mosque. Then an exchange of fire started between Britishers killing Terrorists and Terrorists killing Britishers as if the bullets were raining.

The scary sounds of the bombing were only audible all around. Once it became so difficult that they were not able to get out of their apartment.

In such an environment Gangu joined the college. Every teacher was given a class and Gangu was in charge of one of the classes. The students were all girls. They were so adorable and kind Gangu used to love spending time with them. Likewise, Gangu created such a friendly bond with them whenever she used to wear some saree which they didn't like. They would say to her, Don't wear this saree, it doesn't look good. They used to admire their teacher.

As the college was international there was the faculty from different countries. It was a pleasure to interact with the different nationalities for Gangu. The violence levelled up, and they started entering college and killing the teachers. One of the teachers was killed on the spot; he was British by nationality.

Everyone was running helter-skelter but the students of Gangu were protective. The moment they knew about the incident. They said Gangu, we won't let anything happen to you. They make a huge circle asking her to be in the center to protect her.

There was also a fight among the terrorist groups going on. Each new day would begin with the death of near and dear ones. The students of Gangu would say, yesterday I lost my uncle and so on. In this restless situation, Gangu has to leave her son behind and get into the work. Just as usual her husband would not bother anything.

Once Gangu was to visit the education ministry in this terrifying situation. Gangu took the car and went off to the ministry. There were many security check posts in between the roads. They were so strict that they would ask the people to get down and check them separately. Each and everything inside the car as well as the people traveling in the car first check deeply.

At one of the check ports, Gangu finds something strange. As women were checked by women only Gangu was standing in the queue. Gangu was surprised to see that one of the girls from her college was there at the security port. Looking at Gangu the girl recognizes that she is from college and even Ganga recognizes her too.

Gangu commanded her, don't worry!

You do your work and do whatever you want to do.

Gangu added, don't be scared. I won't let anybody know that. You do your job!

As soon as Gangu was done with the checking she was left to go to her destination.

Each day the conflict was worse. There was no hope for what would happen next. Terrorists occupied every building setting their base to shoot the British. They occupy the entire Serra Island. People were dying in huge numbers. Serra Island was turned into a battlefield. The war carried on day and night. The survival of civilians was at stake. Gangu was alone in the apartment with her child. As Gangu's terrace was very close to the sea, terrorists had made their base on the top of the terrace to fire. The whole wall of Gangu's apartment was full of bullet marks. Mother's love is always great. Gangu puts the baby under the bed covered with lots of pillows and cotton surrounding so that the intensity of the bullet can be reduced.

Deep inside Gangu thought that she wouldn't survive. Gangu told her brother-in-law, if I don't survive, then send my baby to my parents. They will look after him.

Each day her apartment neighbors would die due to being hit by a bullet. Once the tragedy was above to happen thank God they were saved. The bullet came and hit the man who was staying downstairs. The moment the terrorist came to know that one of the residents was injured by the bullet. They came running to apologize and stopped firing. But things were still going on as Seera Island was a huge landscape Gangu was terrificed after that event.

Similarly, they were completely alone Aden was cut off completely from the world. No newspapers were rustling on the doorstep and no letters arriving from far away. No plane were runnning they lived in a bubble, isolated from the rest of the world. This seclusion gnawed at them, their fears reverberating in the silence. Gangu's family in India must have fantasised about the worst-case situations because they couldn't contact them. Their thoughts, fuelled by silence, may have constructed a bleak picture of Gangu. an unknown fate on this remote island.

Suddenly one night the rumor was the war stopped. There was haunted dark and frightening silence. Next, it took a horrifying turn there was a terrifying rumbling sound. Gangu went to see on the balcony what was happening she saw the Irish Army with huge bloodcurdling tanks rolling on the bridge. Gangu was scared as no one was with her. There were her friends in the next building. Suddenly the rumbling sound stops. Gangu tried to go to the next building as it was dark assuming nobody would see her.

As soon as she stepped out of the apartment someone just jumped from the tank and hit her with the gun.

He said, stop don't move.

He terrifyingly asks her, where are you going?

Gangu replied while shivering, I stay here and I just thought to go to my neighbour.

He commanded, Go back home!

Gangu not giving a second thought ran steadily from there. He came following her up to her house's door as she entered he went back.

The next day all troops came by tank. They just thought that terrorists were hiding in the buildings. They started their operation of fetching them but the terrorists had left the island long saying they didn't want to hurt the civilians. The troops kept on searching they went to every room. Gangu was alone with the child. They were checking every corner whether there was a bomb or weapons with them. Like all other rooms, they came to check Gangu's room.

Suddenly the troops knock on the Gangu's door. Gangu's heart started pounding with fear. Her mind was flooding with too many thoughts, thinking the door would last day of life. She has no other option but to open the door. In both ways, the sword of death was hanging for them.

Gangu hiding the fear, opened the door with shivering hands. There were three of them. They were tall, gigantic bodies wearing troops' uniforms. On top of it, they wear a massive helmet bigger than their face. As soon as they entered they went on checking every corner of the house— kitchen, bedroom, bathroom and so on. They didn't leave any objects they opened the bottles, boxes, and photo frames cruelly messing the whole house. But couldn't find anything as innocent civilians.

Children tend to be unexpected. Vikram proceeded to play with the soldiers. Gangu, standing trying to stay calm as well as worried while Vikram smiling, giggling and playing with troops.

Suddenly, one of the soldiers began speaking, as if it had come to life. "I have a son just like him," thinking of his own family.

The soldier kept talking, telling anecdotes of his son's mischievous exploits, while Vikram remained focused on his game, unconscious of the amazing scene developing around him.

Gangu kept quiet but deep inside saying, your work is done please go from here.

After the search operation of terrorists, everything turned black and quiet. Gangu was shut off from the rest of the world for a gruelling 36 hours when the electricity and water failed. She couldn't see anything, and there was just the sound of her breathing. It was a terrible period, but Gangu made it through. Around the same time, Aden won independence, and the city grew rapidly, soon evolving into a modern one. Even though his surroundings were constantly changing, Gangu would always remember those long, quiet hours of effort. They served as a reminder of her courage and will to live.

After Aden got its independence a notice that the civilians to clear of dues and outstanding. Gangu managed to pay off the debts and was puzzled about what to do next. As Gangu worked for the British Government. Gangu shipped all the things to India to Bombay. But she is unfortunate that she can't go to India because exodus from Nigeria to Indian.

Meanwhile, Gangu would visit the Indian Embassy regularly to check the updates to get back to her hometown in India. While Gangu's husband was least bothered. He would be in the house comfortably. On the other hand, the brother-in-law was very smart. He just migrated to the UK before Aden became independent. Even if the passport got canceled in the UK they will issue a new passport in the UK. Learning from brother-in-law Gangu told her husband to do the same but her husband doesn't care and goes on doing what he wants.

While leaving Aden Gangu couldn't leave peacefully. The income tax department caught Gangu. There she came to know that her husband never paid any tax to the government. Luckily she got the gratuity from that money and she paid all the dues of her husband. She kept the money for his tickets and paid advance rent for one month as he came after her.

# CHAPTER THIRTEEN

# Struggle to get Back to the Country

Suddenly one day an Air India plane was coming to survey whether it was safe or not. There were many Indians who were disconnected from near and dear ones. As soon as Gangu knew she rushed there, fortunately, she got a few connection with Air India people so she managed to come back to Bombay along with her child. Soon after landing Gangu was unaware of what to do as she had no contact number of anyone. Air India staff were kind. After landing they arrange for a booking in a hotel room and also alert her not to talk to strangers as people are not good.

Gangu was afraid but she stayed in the hotel room for a night. Then Gangu took the courage to search for her uncle number Gangu took the brave step. There was a big volume of telephone directories in each hotel room. Gangu started search the Uncle's number by his name who was at Bombay.

After the hard work of long hours, Gangu finally found the contact number of Uncle. As soon as she got the number she connected with him. Gangu's heart was pumping so fast as if it would come out as a telephone ring was going on.

As soon as Uncle picked up the call Gangu told him, I am Gangu.

Uncle was in shock and replied, where are you?

As they left the hope that Gangu was alive it was a miracle for them.

Gangu narrated, I managed to come back by Air India. They landed me in a hotel in Bombay and gave him the address.

Uncle calms Gangu by saying, stay there I am just driving to pick you up from there.

It took him one and a half hours to reach the hotel. As soon as she saw Gangu he was thrilled.

Uncle told Gangu, I just thought that you are no more and looking at you is making me so delighted.

The tears of joy were flowing in Uncle and Gangu's eyes. Uncle took Gangu to his house. While reaching the uncle's house Aunty was waiting restlessly to see Gangu. As she saw Gangu was at peace and in joy. They had a good conversation for long hours. It was the first trip of Vikram to India. Uncle tries to get Vikram towards him but Vikram doesn't go as they are new people for him.

Gangu asked Uncle, To manage the tickets she wanted to meet her parents.

Gangu added, don't give a message to my parents that I am alive.

Uncle just nodded his head but he had the telegram message send Gangu's parents saying, Gangu is alive! Back in Bombay, You will meet her soon.

As Gangu came to know about the telegram message.

Gangu asked Uncle, why did you send the message to Father? I wanted to surprise them.

Uncle replied to Gangu, I understand their situation. They are worried!

Meanwhile, the parcels which Gangu had sent before from Aden had arrived and were at the dock. Gangu went to get them from the dock along with Uncle. While looking at the parcel Gangu was sad as parcels were opened. Things were missing and heavy demurrage to pay.

Gangu asked the authority, "Why are there holes in the boxes?

They replied Gangu, it was all because of rats in the ship.

Anyhow it is difficult to digest as it seems that holes were made up of humans.

Well, Gangu just kept quiet as coming for the mouth of the dead was the biggest achievement. Afterwards, Uncle helped her to send all the boxes to Mysore and Madikeri by transport.

# CHAPTER FOURTEEN

# Meeting Parents After Years

While getting an air ticket was difficult at that time, there was only one airline operating as domestic . Somehow Uncle managed it and Gangu got the ticket. It took 2 or 3 days to get the tickets. Gangu got the ticket from Bombay to Bangalore. After she landed in Bangalore she had no idea how to commute to Mysore than Madikeri.

As Gangu never traveled before alone it was a new experience for her. There was her elder sister-in-law in Bangalore. She doesn't have any idea how to reach her place nor does she have her contact number. Anyway, the life of Gangu was full of experiences like that it became one of the new experiences for her. As she reached Bangalore she inquired and came to know that there was a bus and night which would drop her to Mysore.

While her son was so supportive he didn't give her any trouble travelling. Only the thing is that Gangu gave him a bottle of juice and cheese all over the journey and he was in his own world. Gangu took the bus and went to Mysore. It was 9 o'clock night by that time she reached.

After reaching Mysore Gangu got puzzled again; she was not aware of how to commute to her in-law's place. Then she started enquiring about whether there was any bus for Madikeri. The next bus in the morning to Madikeri. Waiting till morning was not possible for Gangu so she tried to fetch a taxi.

Luckily Gangu got a taxi from Mysore to Madikeri. Gangu knew multiple languages; she knew Kannada, Tamil, English, Malayalam and Hindi and after visiting Aden she knew a bit of Arabic.

The taxi driver was a kind man. He was speaking with her in Kannada language throughout the journey.

He was saying, Gangu that no one took a taxi this late, especially a woman. It was month of july and dark night raining heavily with lightning and thunder. Gangu travelled through the forest which was silent yet terrifying.

Gangu couldn't narrate her journey to everyone so she kept quiet.

Gangu's father has retired and they have shifted from where they used to live before. Again Gangu was not aware of that place but as the place was popular Gangu just took the name.

It was sharp at night around 2 o'clock in the morning Gangu reached her father's house. As they heard the sound of the horn the lights were turning on of the bungalow. It was the grand entry everyone was at the door waiting for her. As the door was open Gangu found each and everyone standing there and patiently waiting for her. Father, mother, grandfather, brother and servant were all in tears after watching her. They had almost left the hope that she was alive. It was Vikram's first visit to her to his maternal side. After seeing Vikram their happiness was doubled.

Father thanked the taxi driver and asked him to stay at night.

The taxi diver thanked the father for the opportunity and went off.

The taxi driver was a kind man and he safely brought Gangu. There are good people in this world.

Gangu got some relief for a few days following the unpleasant experience. Though life continued to be a struggle, she found meaning in taking care of her child. Her baby was her entire world, and providing him best became her purpose in life. She encountered

new problems every day, but she never gave up. Meanwhile, Gangu stayed in her parent's home to figure out what to do next.

# CHAPTER FIFTEEN

# New Wave of Sorrow.....

Gangu's life has been a roller coaster ride which consists of unexpected turns and scares. Coming back to India was the biggest struggle for Gangu but somehow she managed to and bravely come back. Gangu was in trauma for many days. Every day she would remember the dreadful events that have happened in her life.

In fact, at one time Gangu left the hope that she would survive as the conflict was getting intense. Lovely Seera Island was turned into a bloody battlefield.

Of course, everybody was happy after seeing her after many years as well as coming back from a tragic conflict. Gangu's father's friends would address her Jhansi ki Rani. Everyone was so delighted to see her. A thorn pricking on her foot would cause trouble for her family. They used to keep her on eyelids. Whatever she would ask was made available at the time. But Gangu's crooked man has made her a slave. Little Gangu has grown up and she knows to cover hurt tears.

Likewise, when she connected with family again she was calm. Wiping everybody's tears and saying I am alive. I am with you. Mother looking at her bravery she said, You are not my daughter, you are someone else. It was difficult and shocking the change in Gangu. Anyway after marriage she has made the distance between sky and land all alone.

Meanwhile, the tragic event of Aden was part of her life as well as marrying the most undeserving man. After returning to her parents' house Gangu has spent more than six months at their house. She was mentally disturbed. She wanted to have mental peace. She wanted to bring joy to her life as well as to her baby while being independent. She does not want to live a miserable life again. Meanwhile, parcels have arrived at her parent's house as the uncle gave the address. One of the parcels went to her in-law's place as it contained their address. In that parcel, Gangu has packed all the things in one box which are of them. She doesn't want to take anything which reminds her of them

Meanwhile, life was going on.

Once Gangu's mother asked, How is your husband? Is he good?

Gangu replied He has nothing I have to earn to provide for him. They narrated the story in the best way. Gangu's mother was silent and didn't give much attention to it.

Furthermore, Gangu came to know her husband is back in Mysore with his parents. Gangu knew money by this time his money might got over. He was at his parents' house. Meanwhile, Gangu made the decision that she wanted to live a better life. She wanted to be independent and live her dream life. She wanted to end the tortures and atrocities of her life. Gangu wanted to get a divorce.

While being clear about what would be the next chapter of her life, Gangu moves towards her father to disclose her decision.

'Papa get me some job over here. I want to work, Gangu told her father

Gangu added I want to live with you and get a divorce from him.

As soon as Gangu took the name of divorce her father suddenly said, I am not telling you to go and live with him. You can stay with me. I will look after you and your child.

Gangu's father added that I will admit him to a good school. You don't worry about it, just don't get a divorce!

Everyone will comment that Dr Subbaya's daughter has done this, and everyone will get a new topic to talk about. Instead, you stay with us but don't get a divorce.

*What the world would say,*
*While parting away,*
*Marriages cannot be broken even if it has taken a haunted way,*
*A Girl dying in sorrow each day,*
*But who cares,*
*The only thing is what the world would say?*

Divorce was the biggest taboo in society. Usually like always women are blamed for divorce and given derogatory remarks. The whole girl's family becomes the talk of the town.

Listening to Father Gangu was dicey, what to do next? One of the bank managers has kept the job ready for Gangu in Madikeri Gangu knew that her father would not agree she would go to work from his house. It would go against his name and pride. Gangu was thinking about how she had spent a couple of months. Meanwhile, Gangu wrote a letter to her uncle who was in Bombay. In that Letter, Gangu told the oceans of thoughts going on in her life. Asking for his advice on what to do and where to go.

As days passed Gangu received the uncle's letter which stated if you are ready to settle in Bombay I will arrange for a job in no time. Just think that job is ready only, Uncle added. Need your confirmation that you are onboard for the job.

It was a great opportunity for Gangu. Being in Bombay sky is no limit. Gangu was anxious to ask for permission. Giving liberty to go to another city will take her away from their clutches. She would be a bird doing whatever she wants. Gangu was perplexed to decide. She wanted fertile soil to sow herself to grow.

In the Interim Gangu's brother has come for holidays. He was studying engineering and was staying in a hostel. They had a unique sibling bond. They would share each and everything with each other. Her brother was dearest to her.

Gangu narrated that she has got an opportunity to work in Bombay referenced by Uncle. Gangu's brother was delighted after hearing about the opportunity.

Gangu's brother said, Take up the job. You stay here you will be under Dr Subbaya's name only. You will not get any freedom. They still think you are an unmarried girl studying in college.

Gangu's brother added, take up the job they want to keep you under control. You go to Bombay and spread your wings.

Gangu's brother was in his fourth year of engineering. You go there after completing engineering I will stay with you. Don't worry Gangu's brother gave assurance.

This is the golden opportunity Uncle has given you to grab it! He added.

Convincing the parents was a hectic job, meanwhile, Gangu's mother fell ill and she was admitted to nearby hospital and father was along her. Gangu and her brother were handling all the house chores. In the meantime, the uncle sent her the joining letter and asked to go to Bombay for an interview. It was a name-sake interview only the thing Gangu was to say yes or no.

While her brother was so supportive he told Gangu, I will say to father and mother at the hospital and convince them.

Meanwhile, after the brother's support, Gangu boosted her confidence.

Gangu told Uncle, I am coming to Bombay. At the same time Gangu, being excited, started packing her bag.

The brother went to the hospital and told his father, enough is enough to let her go. I want Gangu to be independent. Let her be strong by standing firmly on her feet. I will travel along with her to Mangalore and board her Bombay flight.

*Why women's dreams are difficult to achieve,*
*When the sky is one to achieve,*
*Why is one bird in the cage while another is expanding its wings,*
*Why is one burden off while the other can achieve anything?*
*Why the journey of one is difficult when the destination is easy,*
*Why are so many pebbles in the way of a girl's victory...*

Gangu's brother added I will take care of the child, you don't have to worry till the time Gangu comes back. And if you want to stay in the hospital please stay. He took leave for the college. During the same time when Gangu was planning to commute her parents came back from the hospital.

The father was angry, scolding and yelling. But this time is for independence Gangu stayed strong and didn't react as if she had turned her feelings to stone.

As promised, the brother came to drop her till Mangalore and from Mangalore the Gangu took the flight to Bombay. Throughout the travelling Gangu was worried about her child. She was helpless as she didn't have another option. Landed in Bombay with a kind gesture, uncle was there to pick her up at the airport and she stayed there at her uncle's house during the visit. Gangu went for an interview and got selected. The joining of the job was up to her whenever she wanted, therefore Gangu went back to Madikeri. Father was annoyed with her and didn't talk much to her but Gangu was solidified on her decision. Her brother took care of her son till the time Gangu got settled properly in Bombay.

# CHAPTER SIXTEEN

# Journey of Reaching Next Destination

The life of Gangu was taking a drastic change. Gangu was delighted to open her wings to fetch the freedom she always wanted. Bombay city is known as its city of dreams and carrying such a dream Gangu went to Bombay. Gangu even realized when Bombay made her part of them. Gangu flew from Madikeri to Bombay with countless hopes for a better life.

It was July, and the sky was full of dark, dense clouds that prepared to pour. The air was thick with humidity, and the prospect of a deluge hovered in the air. Occasionally, a distant rumbling of thunder could be heard, indicating the oncoming storm. Trees swung gently in the air, their leaves rustling as if to reveal secrets. The streets were calm, with few people.

Till the time Gangu reached the Mangalore airport, it was pouring rain heavily.

As the plane flew from the runway. The weather made a dramatic shift as heavy rain fell from the dark, gloomy clouds overhead. Thunder rumbled loudly, reverberating throughout the sky and contributing to the ominous mood. At the same time, turbulence fiercely rocked the plane, forcing nervous passengers to grasp their seats firmly. The mix of heavy rain, thunder, and turbulence made for a frightening and uncomfortable experience for everyone on board. It was a horrifying journey in the sky. It was just like the lightning hitting the plane. Many of the passengers were fainting and vomiting.

As the plane was about to land in Bombay. Pilots receive a message that they can't land in Bombay due to flooding. So the flight was diverted to Pune. The condition of Pune was the same as Bombay. Again the flight was diverted to Ahmedabad. All the passengers started panicking after that. Some were scared and into tears throughout the journey. Passenger started vomiting and fainting. Looking at the condition of the passengers, the cabin crew started to get worried and one of the cabin crew fainted. While other cabin crew started to get worried.

Gangu was calm, whatever had to happen would happen. As one of the cabin crew sat with Gangu.The cabin crew found her brave and she was saying we are running out of fuel as well as crying. Luckily the weather was better in Ahmedabad. It was just drizzling in Ahmedabad and landed safely. The airline was arranging for a hotel for them to stay, meanwhile, pilots received a message that they could land in Bombay.

As soon as they got the update they boarded the plane and reached their destination Bombay safely. After landing Gangu went outside to catch the vehicle to reach her uncle's house. As soon as she came out of the airport Bombay was turned into a ghost town. Nothing was there outside, not a bus or taxi. Everything was flooded.

As all roads were flooded. Gangu's Uncle was unable to pick her up from the airport. All the passengers had someone with them while Gangu was only travelling alone.

Looking at Gangu one of the pilots came and asked, how will you go? There is no one with you and there is no transportation either.

There was one of the couples who was waiting for the driver to come with the car as soon as he heard the pilot saying that they had come forward. The wife was so gentle that she volunteered to give a ride to Gangu wherever she wanted to go.

She told the pilot, don't worry, I will take her and we are with her. Thankful Gangu had Uncle's address written in the diary. Her uncle was staying at Sion.

There was dreadful water logging at Sion. The water logging was almost touching their neck.

The driver was a kind man. He parked the car far away where there was not much waterlogging. He took all the luggage of Gangu on the head and both of them waded through the filled neck-deep water streets. It took them almost 1 hour to reach her uncle's place. It was early morning at 5 o'clock. Finally, Gangu reaches to uncle's place. The driver kept all the luggage and vanished away before they could thank him.

As soon as Uncle saw Gangu was coming his tears just flooded out.

He told Gangu, I just thought that I had lost you. How will I answer Dr Subbayya? Where is their daughter?

He added I must not have called you to face such a dreadful situation. While continuously crying.

Gangu replied, don't worry uncle, I am here in front of your eyes. I am alive.

It was not at all easy to reach Bombay but Gangu managed it due to her bravery. Gangu has been seeing terrifying situations so often that it was just normal for her. That was the beginning of the Bombay journey for Gangu.

# CHAPTER SEVENTEEN

# Learning to live in the City of Dreams—Bombay

Bombay is often called the city of dreams, yet achieving those dreams can feel as elusive as catching the moon. Turning dreams into reality in Bombay demands relentless struggle and hard work. Gangu was a formidable fighter, embracing challenges with unwavering resilience. Despite the hardships, bravery sometimes seemed lost. Nonetheless, she persevered. Gangu's journey was a testament to her enduring spirit amidst Bombay's demanding landscape. In a city where dreams require immense effort, her story highlighted the strength needed to pursue aspirations against all odds, showing that even in the face of adversity, the determination can lead to success.

Gangu was not sure what would happen in Bombay, but she hoped for the best. As she packed her possessions, her heart was filled with both joy and dread. The city of dreams enticed her with the promise of new beginnings and prospects. She couldn't help but anticipate the opportunities that awaited her in the busy metropolis. Despite the uncertainties, Gangu maintained optimism. She was confident that her hard work and commitment would pave the path for a better future. With a deep breath and a hopeful smile, she set out on her trek, eager to see what Bombay had in store for her.

While at Madikeri the nasty man whom she had got married was not leaving her. He used to visit her father's place and create issues or conflicts. He landed in India at his father's house. His parents were frustrated with him, the same thing he used to do with his parents. He would go out at night and come home the next day. He would not provide any penny to them. His parents just raised their hands saying, we can't keep you in the house

They also added you are not giving any penny for household expenses.

And with the frustration they just throw him out of the home.

He went to Bombay to his sister's home and stayed with her which Gangu did not know. Once he had to come to Madikeri he was whole night fighting with Gangu. Gangu's Brother could hear in his room. His sibling love arose. He knocked at the door and said, If you don't stop fighting I will break the door and throw you out of the house. He also warned by the morning I should not see you in the house. If I see you I will throw you out of house but he left in the morning.

Gangu couldn't understand the game of fate. Life had thrown so many hurdles at her, each one more tough than the last. Following the dreadful tragedy, she found herself dealing with the twists and turns that fate had in store. It was as if the world was playing a cruel game with her, testing her courage and fortitude at every turn. Gangu frequently pondered why she had to go through such pain. What was the reason for these trials? The game of fate remained a perplexing mystery, but Gangu's everlasting love for her kid kept her going, hoping for a better tomorrow.

Before Gangu would reach Bombay he was already there. As he was thrown from his father's house he was staying at his sister's house in Bombay. Gangu was unknown for the game he was plotting against her. He went to her uncle and told him, I wouldn't do it again. I want to live a better life with Gangu again. Somewhere uncle came into his words and he found that he genuinely felt sorry from inside. Animals don't change even if they are adapted likewise he was the same.

As soon as Gangu reached Bombay she asked her uncle to get an apartment for rent. It was an easy job for her uncle as he has good contacts across the city. Gangu's uncle managed to find one at Mahim. It was located in a prime location where the facilities of transportation were quite easy to get. The railway station was just a few steps away as well as the bus stand. Gangu tried to make a place in the city of dreams. She joined the office as well. The company was a public limited company. She was appointed to the accounts department under the head of a lady who was CA. The equation between both of them was not good, the lady was not so friendly and she had some jealousy issues. Gangu just carried on as she wanted to be independent.

Gangu's past collided with her present one day, threatening to destroy the little calm she had managed to create. Her heart skipped a beat as she noticed her husband and uncle waiting at the entrance. Gangu took him inside the house as he was with her uncle. Her Husband had falsely convinced the Uncle that he had changed.

Uncle told Gangu, to give him a second chance he has changed.

He added I will give the job to him in my factory. Don't worry!

Gangu's uncle was a prosperous businessman who ran a major factory in Thane. Gangu's uncle recognised the need to support his family and provided Gangu's spouse with a position at his factory. It was a show of love and responsibility, ensuring that Gangu's husband could support his family. Gangu's family felt more stable and hopeful after working.

Keeping the word of Uncle Gangu gave the wicked man another chance. Gangu has made the flat agreement on his name. For he would sense some responsibility though she was paying the rent. Meanwhile, Gangu urged her brother to send Vikram to Bombay. A mother's heart was aching to see her son. the Gangu's brother made all the required arrangements and boarded Vikram to Bombay. Gangu was ecstatic to see her kid after so many days away. When she finally saw him, her heart melted at the sight of his sweet, innocent face. Vikram has always been a pleasant and well-behaved child, never causing any problems while growing up. His innocent and adorable personality made Gangu's heart trouble even more for him. The notion of him suffering any pain or misery was heartbreaking to her.

Life was difficult in Bombay for Gangu. Surviving in the city of Bombay is difficult. The only friend that Mumbaikar have is "Mumbai local" popularly known as the lifeline of Mumbaikar. Maximum working professionals had to make the journey from home to the office from the local. Sometimes it is packed with crowds while sometimes there are few places to breathe. Gangu too made Mumbai a local part of her life. She would travel to the office by Mumbai local. Gangu has never used a public vehicle in her life. Before in Aden, she travelled to work by car. But time is the best teacher. Gangu adapted to the Mumbai lifestyle. In the beginning, Gangu didn't know how to get on the train. She would climb the train with the push of the crowd and get down with the push of the crowd. Gangu would get anxious but she learned over time.

While her husband has never changed a bit he was the same wicket man. Like a Chameleon has started showing his true colours. He went for the job for a few days, ended up fighting with other employees of the factory and stopped working. Again depended on the money on Gangu. His aggression and guiltlessness arose again as Gangu had made the housing agreement in his name. He would say, get out of my house, this is my house. And take your child also. He has no affection towards the child also. She made the agreement in his name thinking he would feel responsible but Gangu was paying the rent which her father was sending.

Meanwhile, Gangu was enjoying the new work environment. The major problem Gangu faced was language. As in Bombay most of the people would be Marathi. Gangu was not at all aware of the alphabet of Marathi. But she managed somehow. There was a mixed work culture. Some of them were very good with her while some of them had some jealousy issues with her. The top level of the company such as the MD and advisors would appreciate her contribution to the company and consider Gangu as an asset to their company. Gangu gave her 100% in whatever work have was given. Due to this, it has helped the company in progress as well as creating goodwill.

Gangu has a brilliant grasping power. Once a company secretary was appointed Gangu was assigned the duty to give the briefing about the share of the company. As it was ordered by the higher authority Gangu accepted the duty. Gangu was not aware of the share market at all but she took this duty as a new opportunity of learning. She started getting books related to the share market and would prepare important pointers to explain the next day to the company secretary. thankful to her grasping power she learnt it deeply and became master of it. Meanwhile, Gangu was also doing a company secretary course from the British Institute which she didn't complete. Gangu updated herself wherever she could and focused on her career of lifting. She was devoted and hard-working.

Meanwhile, her husband was again taking his evil root. He would go to work for someone in one place and end up having conflicts. In the beginning, he had worked at a few places. But the reason for leaving the job was always the same: he would do the conflict in the company. Disturbing the peace wherever he went was part of his nature. After that, he never tried searching for a job and would stay back at home. Life of Gangu was taking the same turn as it was before.

While Gangu's uncle would get upset seeing him at home. He would come to Gangu's house and guide him many times. But the uncle's words would not make any difference to Gangu's husband.

Finally, one day Gangu told his uncle, that to leave him uncle he wouldn't change nor would you be able to change.

She added I am only with him just because of you. While Gangu's husband was least bothered by what anybody would say. Gangu just thought it was part of life and went on.

# CHAPTER EIGHTEEN

# Dismiss of Beloved-Brother

Gangu took refuge in her son Vikram, who provided her with hope in life. Life in Bombay was a rollercoaster ride, with everyone always on the move and little time to relax. The early days were especially taxing, but Gangu persevered through it all. She confronted each hurdle with resolve and resilience, knowing she had to persevere for Vikram's sake. Despite the city's unrelenting speed and heavy expectations, Gangu found courage in her maternal love and the prospect of a better future for her kid among the buzzing chaos of Bombay.

Suddenly one day a heartbreaking event took place in Gangu's life. As usual, Gangu was in a mess of preparing for her day. It has been a week since Vikram arrived. Out of the blue, a dreadful telegram unaware of the horrifying news that was about to be told to Gangu. Gangu went to pick up the call. As soon as Gangu heard the news she was shattered into pieces. Her brother has made a journey to heaven. Gangu was blank after listening to it. Everything around her just became dark for her.

Her brother was going to college after vacation. While travelling back to the college he met with an accident. He died on the spot due to internal bleeding. Brother was the biggest support for Gangu; he was the reason for her to migrate to Bombay. Gangu loved him so much being an elder sister he was like a kid to her. All the family members were at the great loss of their beloved son. It was a shock and painful to dismiss a dear one at such a young age.

Gangu was so devastated after this accident she would'nt not like to live in Bombay. The parents were at a great loss and their physical health was not keeping up due to it. Gangu was mentally disturbed and wanted to leave Bombay and get back to Madikeri. Being an elder daughter she thought going back to Bombay would give them some support to cope with the loss which all the family had made.

She was all set to leave Bombay. One Uncle came to meet Gangu for condolence. Gangu told her uncle, I am leaving Bombay and going back to Madikeri. My parents need me in this devastating period.

Uncle replied I can understand what situation you are in right now. But I would suggest you not to go back to Madikeri.

He added, your journey is different now you need to stand for yourself. Think about you.

The decision is all yours whatever you choose, he said. But remember one thing finally it is your own hands only which will come under your head. Remember and decide to stay back.

After the conversation with Uncle Gangu changed her mind and decided to stay back in Bombay. The loss which she was unable to recover from. But that is the name of life moving on. Gangu has a special place in her heart for her brother and he will always be there. Gangu was in Bombay due to his unbeatable support. He has always encouraged Gangu to stand for her freedom and expand her wings.

# CHAPTER NINETEEN

# Lovely Memories of Being a Parent!

Gangu was trying to endure the loss of her brother. Her son was like a medicine for wounds. His smile would make her forget sorrow and long conversation would take her into another. Meanwhile, Gangu wanted the admission of her child into school. Gangu was worried as Bombay was a new place for her. She was adapting and she did not know the school there in the locality. Vikram landed in Bombay in September. The academic year had begun long back on the CBSE board.

Gangu was puzzled about what to do and how to admit him to the school. Gangu was in fear that her child might lose one year due to academic month differences. While her husband doesn't have any sense of responsibility.

Gangu would struggle from school to school enquiring about admission. She wanted to have the best school for Vikram so that he would get a quality education. Likewise, once she went to one of the schools they agreed to admission and explained the processes as well. But Gangu found the school not up to the mark so she didn't get his admission over there. However, from somewhere, Gangu came to know about the famous school located in Wadala. But Gangu was unaware of how to get admission there.

Meanwhile, Gangu's relative General was visiting Bombay. He was fond of her son. The General called her and told her he would be at the VVIP lounge at the airport. He wanted to meet her at the airport. She went and met him. He asked her about her son. Then she shared about the problem of school of her son.

Uncle was delighted to see Gangu after many days. As the uncle saw Gangu's husband he took a good class.

He told to Gangu's husband, do you have any shame to do such things to your wife?

Sense some responsibility on your shoulder to go to work, he added. You are a parasite dependent on your wife. Shameless! Scrounging on your wife.

Gangu's husband didn't utter a word and was smiling.

On the other hand, Gangu's uncle gave her a helping hand to ask for anything if she needed. He focused on her to say something she wanted. At present Gangu's need was only to get admission of her child at a reputed school.

Gangu told the uncle, I want Vikram's admission to the school. I am just unable to do so.

Gangu's uncle reacted, Say me the name of the school.

Gangu replied, the name of the school.

Gangu's Uncle, Call them! Take the telephone directory and the school's contact number.

Luckily Gangu found it. As soon as she found the contact number Gangu connected with them.

Hello, I am Gangu, would you please connect the call to the principal of the school? General wanted to talk to him, Gangu said.

The receptionist connected the call to the Principal.

I am General speaking to you. I want my grand nephew to be admitted to your school. I have heard a lot about school and was impressed, Uncle said.

The Principal said, send the child along with his mother and a letter signed by you tomorrow.

The principal added I will admit him.

Gangu was dancing with joy after the telephone conversation. Finally, there was hope to get admission.

Being cheerful Gangu started thanking Uncle again and again.

Her uncle told her to keep quiet and asked her to go tomorrow for admission. He gave her a letter signed by him.

Gangu couldn't sleep that night due to joy and excitement. She was waiting for tomorrow morning to get her child admitted to school. Early in the morning Gangu wakes up the child and dresses him up for an interview. As soon as they had breakfast they went for an interview. Finally, they reached. Gangu saw the school for the first time. The school's infrastructure was outstanding. It consists of a huge ground, prayer room, auditorium, classrooms and so on. Gangu reached the school before the time of the meeting hence they were asked to wait in the lobby.

After a few minutes, they were called into the Principal's cabin. Gangu was excited. The Principal was a kind man. He was an Italian man. He had a blue glittering eye and a broad smile on his face. Gangu gave the letters signed by the General to the Principal.

The Principal asked a few questions to Vikram like, what is your name?

Who are you? What is your mother's name? What is your father's name? Where do you live?

Vikram would answer the question within a fraction of a second confidently. Icing on cake he also recited a poem.

The Principal appreciated Vikram and was impressed by him. At that time Gangu was sitting next to Vikram feeling proud of his confidence. Meanwhile, this is all because of his maternal grandmother. She had taught him many things when he was at Madikeri hence he spoke.

The Principal told Gangu, to admit your child today itself and called the teacher of the nursery.

Admit this child into Senior Kg, the Principal told the teacher.

Upon listening teacher reacted, Sir my students have learnt so much. This boy didn't know how can he be admitted to senior Kg.

I can sense this child has good grasping power. Don't worry he will catch up fast, the Principal told the teacher.

Agreeing with the Principal went for further procedure as directed by the teacher.

Finally, tomorrow, Gangu's child will join the class. Gangu was top of the world after the completion of the admission process. Gangu was thankful to her uncle and God due to which admission of Vikram was possible.

Gangu completed all of Vikram's shopping on the way home from school. She got him a new school bag, a water bottle, a tiffin box, a compass box, and all the necessary stationery. Gangu felt relieved and satisfied after ensuring Vikram had all he needed for school. It was a long day, but her efforts paid off when she was able to get Vikram admitted to the school. Gangu felt relaxed for the first time in a long time. Seeing her kid ready and equipped for his schooling offered her a ray of hope and satisfaction amid her challenges.

Gangu sent an emotional letter to her uncle shortly after Vikram was admitted to school. Gangu expressed her heartfelt gratitude and appreciation for his assistance and leadership in the letter. She also supplied Vikram's school address, wanting to keep him updated on his progress. A few days later, her uncle wrote to the principal, praising him for admitting his grandnephew and recognising the school's involvement in Vikram's education. Gangu also formed a positive relationship with Vikram's instructors and the principal. This supportive connection with the school personnel offered her a feeling of security and belonging, knowing Vikram was in capable hands. Her good relationships provided her with comfort and strength throughout a difficult time.

Likewise, Vikram began his academic journey by taking a step up the education ladder. Thankfully there was a bus facility available hence Vikram would go by bus to school. Vikram was a bright child like a mother good at grasping. Furthermore, the struggle of Gangu was going on going for work, managing the whole household and taking care of the child.

# CHAPTER TWENTY

# Violence to the Next Level

Gangu's struggle was relentless and unstoppable. Day after day, she worked tireless hours and struggled to save every money she could. Her troubles were aggravated by her husband's constant domestic violence. His beatings were violent and vicious, leaving her body covered in bruises that became blue and black. Despite the anguish and overwhelming terror, Gangu worked hard to keep her injuries hidden from the outer world, hiding her misery and preserving a false sense of normalcy. Her tenacity was as impressive as it was heartbreaking, demonstrating her unwavering spirit in the face of unimaginable adversity.

Professionally, she was moving forward and making progress, but her personal life was plagued by the same recurrent challenges. She kept her family's problems private, never revealing them to anybody, no matter how serious they were. The contrast between her professional development and her emotional anguish was obvious, but Gangu bore her responsibilities alone in quiet.

Every night, her greedy husband argued with Gangu and demanded money. Despite her best efforts to hide a little to manage the home, her nasty husband would locate and grab everything. His ravenous hunger made Gangu's life a living hell. Every night was a fight since he had no concern for her well-being or hard work. Her efforts to establish stability were continually foiled by his harsh deeds. Despite her professional success, Gangu's personal life was overshadowed by his unwavering brutality, leaving her in despair. The contrast between her professional advancement and her struggles was apparent and devastating.

He used to beat and kick her, but now he strangles her. Gangu's neck became blue from the bruising, and she had a difficult time eating. Despite the increasing violence, Gangu bore it all, believing she had no alternative. She covered the wounds and bruises with her saree, concealing the evidence of her misery from the world. Every day was a fight for survival, but she persevered in quiet. The physical agony was intense, but the mental toll was far more severe. Gangu's fortitude was admirable, even though her position deteriorated by the day.

Her cruel spouse was suddenly stricken with poliomyelitis, a crippling disease. The sickness immobilised his whole body, making him useless. Despite everything she had gone through, Gangu brought him to a private hospital and sought the advice of a specialist. It took 45 days for him to show indications of improvement. While his body remained immobilised, his tongue was unaffected. The horrible man would yell and insult her as loudly as ever. His constant ranting resonated through the hospital halls, and all of the other patients could hear his nasty comments. Gangu felt a great deal of humiliation and embarrassment every time she had to attend the hospital.

Gangu frequently hoped that, like his body, his voice could be muted. She believed it would have been a blessing. The financial strain of her husband's extended hospitalisation was immense, and the money drained away like water. Fortunately, Gangu's father intervened and provided money to cover the medical bills, bringing much-needed financial respite. Despite the constant verbal abuse and financial pressure, Gangu continued to care for her husband, demonstrating a tenacity and perseverance that was both painful and inspiring.

There was no serenity in Gangu's life. Her days were filled with pain and misery, and there appeared to be no end in sight. Fortunately, Gangu had assigned a maid to care for her kid while she was in the hospital. It gave her some comfort to know her kid was in safe hands. Meanwhile, her husband was steadily improving, regaining strength and mobility. His health improved day by day, and he was soon back to normal. Despite her troubles, Gangu took consolation in her son's rehabilitation, which provided a ray of hope in her otherwise unhappy life.

The ungrateful, selfish man ultimately came home. His shameless and heartless demeanour remained constant, and it wasn't long before his aggressive inclinations reappeared. He resumed his aggressive conduct, instilling anxiety and tension in the home. This time, his rage extended to the maid, with whom he constantly argued over petty topics such as food. The man's incapacity to recognise the attention and effort shown by people around him was as obvious as ever.

On one especially horrible day, the man's nastiness reached new heights. Taking advantage of the fact that the home agreement was in his name, despite never having paid the rent himself, he exercised his authority most ruthlessly. In a fit of wrath, he forced Gangu and her kid out of the house, discarding their possessions out of the house.

Despite these terrible blows, Gangu's irrepressible spirit refused to die. She realised she needed to be strong for her child, to create some sense of stability and security in a world that looked persistently cruel and brutal. Her fortitude and courage, while continuously tested, formed the foundation around which she built her determination to overcome the dreadful circumstances she found herself in.

He began pestering Gangu for money again, demanding more and more from her with little concern for her well-being or the difficulties she was already facing. Gangu, looking for a way to cooperate without entirely committing herself, offered to pay him by cheque.

However, her spouse reacted cruelly and cunningly. "Refuse! All I want is cash. He snapped, "My name should not be used anywhere." His demand was more than a desire; it was a deliberate act. He was astute, well aware that cash transactions leave no paper trace, so there would be no evidence that he had taken money from her. This allowed him to continue manipulating and abusing others without fear of being prosecuted.

His split personality exacerbated the situation's uncertainty and danger. He could change from a decent person to a tyrant abuser in a matter of seconds. Gangu lived in perpetual anxiety and uncertainty as a result of this instability, never knowing what to anticipate from one instant to the next. His proclivity for abrupt and severe behavioural swings made her life a living nightmare as she navigated his unpredictable demands and explosive rage.

Gangu's life became an agonising cycle of attempting to accommodate him while shielding herself and her kid from his constant demands. The persistent strain of his harassment exhausted her emotionally and financially, but she persisted because she was determined to ensure her child's safety and future. The continual fear of his tantrums and manipulative techniques kept her on edge, waiting for the next wave of nastiness.

Despite the enormous difficulties, Gangu's perseverance remained her most valuable attribute. She was resolved to outwit her husband's machinations and provide a better life for herself and her child. Every day, she confronted the unthinkable with fortitude, believing that one day they would be free of his tyrannical clutches and able to live in peace and security.

Once, in a moment of desperation, Gangu mustered the courage to tell her husband, "I don't have money to give you." She hoped that this honest admission might temper his relentless demands, but instead, it provoked a response that was both vile and chilling. With an impudent smile, her husband replied, "You are so beautiful. Come on, I will take you to the whorehouse. Men will come and pay you for your beauty." That money you give me.

The evil man's words were like a dagger to Gangu's heart, scattering her composure and leaving her in a state of shock. The sheer depravity of his suggestion was beyond anything she could have imagined. He was not only indifferent to her plight but was willing to degrade and exploit her in the most abhorrent manner possible. The gravity of his cruelty left her speechless and horrified.

Gangu came from a rich and reputed family, where she had been raised with values of dignity and respect. The thought of being subjected to such humiliation was unbearable. Yet, she chose to remain silent, swallowing her pride and dignity to preserve her family's honour. She understood that any resistance or outcry might provoke further abuse or public disgrace, which would only compound her suffering. Parents give their daughters in marriage that man will look after her but he was ready to sell her.

Her silence was not a sign of weakness but a testament to her strength and resilience. She endured his vile proposition with quiet dignity, knowing that her worth was far greater than his demeaning words. This internal fortitude allowed her to maintain a sense of self-worth and integrity, even in the face of such profound degradation.

Despite the darkness that enveloped her life, Gangu's resolve to protect her family's reputation and her child's future remained unshaken. She continued to bear the brunt of her husband's cruelty, her spirit unbroken even as her circumstances grew increasingly dire. Her enduring strength in the face of relentless adversity was a powerful testament to her character, embodying a resilience that could not be shattered by even the most malevolent of forces.

Every day, Gangu fought to preserve her sense of self and the dignity she had been raised with, finding solace in the knowledge that she was protecting her child from the same suffering. Her perseverance, in the face of seemingly insurmountable challenges, underscored a remarkable fortitude that refused to be extinguished by the cruelty of her husband's actions.

He was mad for money. He could do anything for it. His fondness for music had led to a wonderful collection of CDs, which he guarded jealously. One evening, as Gangu returned home from work, she found his friends knocking at the door. There were three of them. Innocent Gangu, always trying to be accommodating, opened the door and invited them in when they asked for the CDs.

"Search and take what you need," she said, gesturing towards the collection.

Meanwhile, his friends had ulterior motives. "We've heard you make an energetic coffee," they said with a smirk. "Your husband told us. Could you make it for us as well?"

Despite feeling uneasy, Gangu complied. She made the coffee and served it to them, unaware of the evil plans they harboured. After drinking the coffee, they left, and Gangu went about her evening, blissfully ignorant of the deceitful machinations unfolding behind her back.

The people in Gangu's colony were caring and helpful, a small comfort in her otherwise troubled life. Among them was a man she regarded as her "Rakhi brother," who lived in the colony and had always looked out for her. One day, as Gangu was climbing the stairs, her Rakhi brother approached her with a concerned expression.

"Did your husband's friends come to your house?" he asked.

Puzzled, Gangu replied, "Yes, they came to take some CDs."

Her Rakhi brother's face darkened with worry. "Don't let them inside again. Your husband sends them to your house in exchange for money. He waits downstairs while they're in your home."

Gangu's heart sank. She realised the depth of her husband's treachery and the extent to which he exploited her trust. Her mind raced as she pieced together the disturbing puzzle. His friends' visits were not as innocent as they seemed; they were part of his sinister schemes to make money off her.

From that moment on, Gangu resolved to be more vigilant, aware that her husband's greed knew no bounds and that she needed to protect herself and her home from his unscrupulous friends. Despite the constant challenges and the dark shadow cast by her husband's actions, Gangu's spirit remained unbroken. Her resilience and newfound vigilance became her armour, allowing her to navigate the treacherous waters of her life with strength and grace.

Gangu was brokenhearted. She had done so much for him, sacrificing her pleasure and well-being to help and care for him. Instead of expressing gratitude, he turned her life into a perpetual burden, leading her to die on the inside every day. Gangu was always depressed as a result of the constant abuse and mistreatment he received. Despite her enormous sorrow, she never confided in anybody about it. She endured her agony in quiet, keeping her pain hidden from the public. His nasty and selfish attitude continued unabated, leaving Gangu feeling imprisoned and helpless, with no end in sight to her ordeal.

Gangu shattered from inside. Her mental health was at the toss as well as physical but Gangu managed it all smiling. Meanwhile, Gangu's husband was so loud and terrifying. The Neighbours would hear the conflicts.

Once the apartment owner where Gangu was staying called her.

He said to Gangu, leave him, why are you enduring? You are educated and independent.

Gangu replied I can't get separated because divorce is a taboo. I have once spoken with my father. He had told me what people would say if you got divorced. My respect!

Forget that all let me talk to your father I will explain to him, owner of the house said.

Leave it! It's all written in my destiny. Thank you for your concern, Gangu told the owner of the house.

But why did you make the housing agreement in his name? the owner asked Gangu.

Gangu replied, I just felt that he would be changed and he would sense some responsibility.

Meanwhile, the days were passing. Getting up, going to work and coming back to endure violence has been a routine. Her health started getting bad and she was diagnosed with high blood pressure because of which she had to take that tablet every day. Whatever her personal life would be she had a mask that hides all. The colony where Gangu resided had about 260 apartments. Vikram had made a lot of friends at the colony. He would go to play along with them at the colony's ground. Due to this eight families become best friends parents as well as children. They would party together and enjoy themselves. While office staff over time differences vanish and everyone becomes good friends. They would hang out for lunch and watch movies together.

*Hours were passing making it into day,*
*Days passed making it into the month,*
*Months passed making it into years,*
*Where is the peace I am waiting for,*
*Even the darkness of night ends with a bright sunny day,*
*When will be darkness of my life turn into light again?*

Meanwhile, her husband would go to community functions and sometimes Gangu also. Once at a community function, Gangu's husband said, I received fifty pounds as a pension.

I give the pension straight to Gangu, he added.

His pension of fifteen pounds! he was full of lies.

# Arrival of the Second Child

In the beginning, Gangu was not in favour of having a second child. As Vikram was growing he ended up making a lot of friends. Each of the friends has their siblings. Observing them Vikram started demanding brother Gangu it was the year 1972. He cried and got crazy to have a brother. Gangu couldn't deny the demand of Vikram. As Gangu used to think Vikram has suffered a lot and he deserves to get happiness. If having a sibling can make him happy then for his happiness she can do anything.

In the year 1973, Gangu came to know that she was expecting for the second time. Gangu was delighted as she thought she could fulfil one of the wishes of her child. Again with a big baby bump, Gangu would go to the office. As Gangu's parents came to know that she was expecting, they were annoyed.

They asked Gangu, why are you having a second child and burdening yourself?

You two are having a miserable life there, why add one more to it, they added.

Gangu just kept quiet because it was the wish of her dear one. Gangu would manage to go for a checkup by herself. She managed to work till the last day before labour pain. The office staff was very supportive. Her manageing director would get scared seeing her working in this condition. Out of concern he would say to Gangu, don't run! Be careful.

Meanwhile, while she was expecting she had a severe jaundice attack. Due to this, she had lost weight. She had become so skinny that only her bones would be visible. She was totally on bed rest. Doctors did their best with trying almost all the medicines but no medicines were making a difference. They lost hope that she would survive. Finally, once her doctor went himself to get the herbal medicine. It was a miracle the herbal medicines were improving her condition. While little Vikram would cry at her side that would break the Gangu more. Gangu would overthink if she died what would happen to her child. Who will take care of him? But God was great.

Luckily her labor pain started at home. She went with her maid to the hospital. There were many complications in delivery since the baby was a breech baby. Gangu fought the complications and delivered a boy again. Thankfully it was a boy since Vikram wanted a brother. He would say to Gangu, if you deliver a girl, don't bring her and give her to someone. I want only a boy.

Gangu's husband and Vikram came to see the baby. The foolish man started fighting at the hospital for the money. His cracked voice was echoing in the hospital. The nurse was angry. The nurse told him, to go away. Do you have a brain where you are?

After listening to the scolding of the nurse, he kept his mouth shut. Vikram saw his little brother and told Gangu, he was not playing with him. he is like a bundle.

Gangu explains to Vikram with affection, he is a newborn. You were also the same when you were born. He will play with you when he grows a bit older.

Vikram went on saying, no he should play now!

Somehow Gangu managed and cooled Vikram.

Gangu named the newborn Vishal. As compared to Vikram Vishal was not at all like him. He was thin and underweight. He would cry and would stay in Gangu's lap for long hours. Meanwhile, the office staff was so supportive the boss himself came to pick her up from the hospital. Gangu went home from the hospital in his car only.

Vishal was a cranky child; mostly he was sick with an upset stomach and wouldn't sleep crying. Gangu would spend the entire night taking him on his lap Meanwhile Gangu got a specialized nanny for Vishal. She was very kind and she had an affection towards Vishal.

Even Gangu's health was getting bad at that time. Gangu was in touch with her brother-in-law. As Gangu was falling sick now her brother-in-law suggested that you need a change. Her Brother-in-law prepared a trip to Zambia. He even sent the tickets to Gangu and her sons. Gangu boarded and went on vacation with her sons.

Zambia is a rich country with a natural landscape. Gangu had a wonderful experience at Victoria Falls. The people of Zambia were heart-warming. Gangu's trip to Zambia was refreshing and calm. Due to this

Gangu's mental health was a bit better.

# CHAPTER TWENTY-TWO

# Disputes of Life.......

As soon as Gangu landed back from Zambia. The owner of the apartment discussed with Gangu that he wanted to sell the flat. If you want you can buy the flat. Of course, Gangu did not want to leave the flat but at the same time, she did not have money as well to buy. Gangu thought of buying a flat she started managing for funds. Gangu asked her father to give her some money to buy a flat while the rest of the money she managed was by loan from the office. She also sells a few gold jewellery which was given as a gift at her wedding. Gangu's father gave her money as well as office authority approved the loan at 18% interest. Somehow Gangu managed to arrange the funds but the biggest problem was that the flat agreement of the house was in the name of husband.

Gangu told the house owner that she wanted to buy property. The house owner was aware of the situation of Gangu and the violence of her husband.

The house owner suggested, that if you are buying the apartment don't disclose it to anyone. Just transfer me the money and I will do all the documentation. Don't worry!

Don't open your mouth to anybody because there are many ill-wishers in society.

Try to search for a flat agreement if you can and destroy it, Owner added.

As suggested by the owner Gangu just kept quiet and didn't let the wall know what was happening meanwhile the owner of the house did all the documentation work.

Finally, one day the owner called Gangu to his apartment and gave her the transferred document and Gangu was the owner of the apartment. The owner of the house was so clever and brilliant that he didn't leave a trace of the activity he had done. Meanwhile, Gangu doesn't express her happiness even after being the owner of an apartment. She just took the transfer certificate and kept quiet.

Meanwhile, as the days went on nobody was aware that the flat was transferred in Gangu's name until one day one of the relatives of the house owner came to know that the apartment sold out. The lady was staying right opposite her building.

As soon as she came to know she disclosed it to Gangu's husband on the street.

Do you know your apartment has been sold? And who took that apartment it's your wife, She said.

As Gangu's husband came to know about that he was boiling with anger.

As he came home he began abusing to the next level. He messes up the entire apartment in search of apartment paper. Meanwhile, Gangu was observing all but didn't utter a word as she knew where the paper was and he wouldn't get them.

After that, Gangu's husband wrote a letter to Gangu's father in which he complained about how Gangu owns property and doesn't let him know.

He also added I am the male of the family she must enquire with me before buying the apartment.

It just hit on the ego of Gangu's husband. He wanted to take revenge on her and cause her immense harm. The next day Gangu was feeding milk to Vishal on her lap. Suddenly the wicked man came with all of his aggression with a thick bamboo stick. On seeing Gangu they didn't give a second thought and started beating Gangu aggressively.

Meanwhile, Gangu was hiding Vishal as he was on her lap. She just bowed down, fully creating a shell to protect Vishal. Frustrated, he kept on beating continuously. While the maid was at the house she tried to stop him but she was unable to. As he was satisfied giving the pain to Gangu he stopped beating her.

# Move of Courage!

Gangu's body was full of marks blue and black. The wounds were deep which needed a doctor. Vishal child specialist was like a friend to her. She went there to dress the wounds. As soon as she saw the wounds she was terrified and somewhere she sensed the violence on Gangu.

She asked Gangu, how did you get such kind of wounds?

While Gangu tried her level best to hide what had happened to her.

Gangu was not replying and indulging her in stories.

The doctor said, tell me the truth, what has happened? Otherwise, I would not dress them.

Somewhere Gangu took the courage and disclosed the violence which had happened to her. The doctor was in tears after hearing about the horrifying violence happening to Gangu.

The doctor said, being an educated woman, why are you bearing so much?

I won't touch you. First, you go to the police station and file a complaint and then to the government hospital.

The doctor came with her to the police station and reported the complaint.

The police staff was so helpful and caring they started to say Gangu, how can you bear this being an educated woman? You must have come here, we are here for you to help you.

They ask the doctor to get back to her clinic while they ask Gangu for a medical report.

Gangu told the police, I will take someone from the office and go to the government hospital.

Gangu took her assistant and driver along with her and went to the government hospital. They were very good to her.

As soon as she got inside the government hospital it was all crowded. Gangu didn't know what to do as she never went to the government hospital. Somehow she did the dressing. One finger of Gangu's hand was fractured. It took a few minutes for them to prepare the medical report. While coming back from the hospital Gangu submitted the medical reports at the police station.

The police gave assurance, don't worry as soon as he comes to the house, just give us a call and we will arrest him.

At the same time, Gangu was saying, Arrest him and don't beat him out of concern

you foolish women, police said to Gangu.

That night he didn't come home. On the next day, Gangu went to the office with all the bandages. As usual, Gangu returned from the office in the evening. As she opened the door of the apartment she found Vikram and maid were getting scared and their faces had turned pale.

Gangu went forward and asked them what happened. Why are you looking like this? Tell me!

As they were frightened they didn't utter a word.

Gangu went to see the other room. She was too shocked. About 15 to 14 men were sitting with her abusive husband. They were those same friends who had evil in their hearts.

The Rakhi brother's advice clicks to Gangu.

Gathering all the courage Gangu told them to get out of my house.

The corrupt friends of her husband told her, this is not your house, this is our friend's house.

On hearing this Gangu reacted, who are you to decide that?

Cruel friends said, we know this is our friend's house, see how he has bashed you. In a vulgar tone.

They were not good by appearance nor by words they seemed to look like thugs. Gangu too got scared. Unaware of what to do. Staying at home was not at all safe for her.

Gangu told the maid and child to stay quietly. I come back in a few minutes.

Gangu ran downstairs to a friend's house who is like a own family.

They were puzzled upon hearing the knocking on the door.

The brother opened the door and asked, what happened Gangu? Why are you so anxious?

Gangu narrated, they are at my home along with my husband. I don't know what to do. She just came running downstairs.

Police have asked me to give a call when he comes to the house, Gangu added.

Showing aggression towards the husband of Gangu, the brother reacted, why are you waiting? Then take my phone and give the call to the police station.

He dialled the number for Gangu. Soon after the phone call Gangu told her brother, let me go upstairs and see what was happening.

Out of worry and care, the brother stopped her from going and said don't go to those thugs alone, wait for me and my wife will come along with you.

Meantime as they were getting out of the house the police reached the colony within 10 minutes. The police squad went to Gangu's house before she reached arrested all of them.

After they got arrested Gangu had a conversation with the police, just give him a warning and don't do anything to them.

Police said, we can't assure you that but we will keep them in lockup one night.

Gangu has earned many good friends in the colony. They were more than a family for her. In every situation, they stand with Gangu hand in hand. As they came to know that man got arrested. They came to Gangu's house to check that she was always alright and Gangu's best friend in the office and her husband so good they would come in midnight to check how she was every night. They stayed far away and still managed to come. Gangu's curiosity arose; she went along with them to the police station to see what was happening there. As soon as they reached there Gangu heard a horrifying sound of argument with police.

They tried to intimidate the police by saying, we have so and so at authority if he comes to know that we have been arrested you will be suspended.

The police said courageously, here is the telephone call whoever you want. Do one thing: call.

Police told Gangu, Mam we won't release them today, they will be released by tomorrow morning. And Gangu went home.

The next morning they were released from the jail and police told Gangu that they wanted to carry on with the case. Meanwhile, Gangu decided that she wanted to separate from the nasty man who had made her life into hell.

Gangu shared the incident with her boss and told her that she wanted to separate from him. She asked the boss to search for a lawyer to fight the case and get the victory.

Meanwhile, She informed her parents by writing a letter. In the letter, she mentions that I am filing a divorce case. If you are with me well and good or I think your daughter is on more.

Her father replied to her through the letter. Due to some ill wishes advice, you are doing so.

The boss was so helpful he found a lawyer for Gangu to fight the case. Gangu had a meeting with a lawyer and gave all the police reports and other information needed. He agreed to fight the case. Unfortunately, after one month the lawyer called the Gangu and said, my heart pains, I can't take any divorce case.

# CHAPTER TWENTY-FOUR

# No Relief from Violence

Gangu endured the passage of time without respite. She was adamant in her desire to leave her husband and live a better life, free of the agony that had consumed her for so long. Unfortunately, she had difficulty finding a solicitor ready to take on her case. Despite her tireless efforts, she encountered various challenges and failures. Gangu worked frantically to win her release, but each attempt was greeted with failure. Her determination, however, remained unwavering, and she continued to dream of a future in which she and her children might live calmly and blissfully.

Meanwhile, they continued to live together, and his aggression remained. Horrifyingly, one day he began strangling Gangu, reaching a new level of agony. Her neck was bruised and darkened, which had unfortunately become a common occurrence. Gangu's health unexpectedly deteriorated. She found it more difficult to carry out her usual duties, particularly walking and climbing. She started having blackouts, which scared Gangu the most.

The physical and mental consequences of the torture were becoming intolerable. Gangu felt imprisoned and helpless to break the cycle of violence. Each day brought new obstacles and concerns, but she was determined to find a way out for the sake of her own and her children's safety

Gangu went to consult the family doctor. The doctor informed Gangu "This is not an ordinary case; you need to consult with a specialist." Advanced testing was required to diagnose the issue. Gangu went to a reputable hospital with all of the necessary facilities and equipment for testing. She met with a specialist, who gave her a brief list of the tests that needed to be performed.

The specialist's suggestion includes a variety of diagnostic tests to determine the severity of Gangu's health difficulties. Gangu had a battery of tests, each aimed at determining the root reason for her declining health.

The procedure was intimidating, but Gangu was determined to discover answers. She thought that a diagnosis would not only throw light on her present health issues but also pave the road for proper treatment and recovery.

Gangu underwent all of the tests prescribed by the doctor and returned with the findings. Gangu was diagnosed with a nodular goitre, which was disrupting blood circulation to her brain, causing her to have blackouts. This diagnosis addressed the difficulty she had been experiencing with daily tasks, particularly walking and climbing stairs.

The doctor explained the ramifications of the diagnosis to Gangu and described a treatment plan to manage her illness. Gangu was happy to finally have answers about her health difficulties, and she was determined to follow the doctor's advice to enhance her quality of life.

The doctor informed Gangu, "You should be hospitalised as soon as possible for this surgical procedure. If left untreated, it may spread and cause other difficulties." Gangu agreed to the doctor's recommendation and was admitted to the hospital. Before the procedure, they ran many tests to see if the goitre was poisonous. Fortunately, the goitre was non-toxic.

Gangu got surgery after completing all of the requirements and examinations. Gangu stayed in the hospital for 15 days after surgery for surveillance. The medical staff attentively watched her growth and addressed any potential concerns.

Meanwhile, they ran tests every day because they were concerned it was cancer. Fortunately, all results were negative, and Gangu showed no symptoms of malignancy.

While she was in the hospital, physicians would ask, "How did this happen to you?" Gangu understood exactly why, but she stayed mute. The physicians would guess, "Something must have happened to you for this to occur."

Gangu has perfected the skill of hiding her family problems. She elected not to reveal the exact reason for her health issue, choosing to keep her personal life private. Her ability to remain calm and withhold information from medical personnel proved her strength and commitment to defend her privacy. Nodule formed due to the strangling of her husband but she didnt disclose it to doctor.

On the penultimate day, around 9 p.m, a doctor came sprinting to Gangu. The doctor screamed with joy, "We don't want to see this beautiful face again—it's all clear!" All of the reports are good, and Gangu is well enough to be discharged."

Gangu felt a surge of comfort and thankfulness wash over her as she absorbed the doctor's words. She had survived a difficult voyage, and now she could look forward to coming home and completing her rehabilitation in familiar circumstances. The doctor's joyous statement signalled the end of a tough chapter in Gangu's life, and she was anxious to leave the hospital.

Meanwhile, Gangu's husband was completely unaware of the difficulties she was experiencing as a result of his actions. Gangu returned to normal life after a few days of recovery, dealing with the typical domestic tensions as well as her workplace responsibilities.

Despite her previous tragedy, Gangu faced the typical obstacles of juggling work and family commitments. She handled her domestic affairs while juggling the demands of her career, all while preserving a sense of normalcy for her children's benefit. However, the recollection of her previous hospitalisation persisted as a sharp reminder of the challenges she had faced. Gangu longed for a break from the upheaval, but she stayed prepared to face whatever problems arose, gaining strength from her tenacity and drive to go forward with her life.

Gangu's husband suddenly experienced a more serious polio neuritis attack. This time, his entire body was paralysed, and he lost his capacity to communicate. Gangu quickly brought him to a specialist, looking for medical assistance. However, the expert declined to accept him, claiming a lack of medical equipment required to treat his illness.

Gangu was once again put in a difficult position, caught between her responsibility to her ailing husband and the necessity to get suitable medical treatment for him. She looked into various hospitals and experts, trying to find someone who could provide him with the essential treatment he required. Despite their tumultuous past, Gangu could not desert her husband in his hour of need.

Gangu was deeply concerned about the magnitude of the situation. She sought to find a solution while dealing with bureaucratic impediments and healthcare system issues. Her husband's deteriorating health left her feeling overwhelmed and confused about where to turn next.

Gangu was forced to move her husband to the government hospital since the essential machinery was only accessible there. Gangu couldn't spend the entire day with him in the hospital because she had to manage both her office and her family. Instead, she hired a servant to look after him throughout the day. Gangu would come in the evenings after work to check on him and make sure he had everything he needed, including his medications.

Gangu struggled to balance work, housework, and care for her spouse. She did her best to balance these tasks, hoping for an improvement in her husband's condition and better treatment from the medical personnel.

Meanwhile, Gangu's father was sending the money quietly for hospital expenses. And the father-in-law plotted a dirty game against Gangu. He sent five hundred rupees for the hospital expenses which was nowhere about 1% of the total expense. Spread the word in the community that he is sending money for his son's treatment and trying to upgrade them in the community. He was a crooked man!

Same as before, after 45 days he recovered from the attack. All the limbs started to show movements and he was all right. The doctor gave him a discharge from the hospital. Gangu took him and came back home.

Gangu was astonished soon after returning from the hospital he was praising Gangu by saying I am alive because of you. Thank you for doing so much!

In the beginning, Gangu just ignored him.

After a few weeks, Gangu said, I have one request if you feel I have done any good to you and you are appreciating please relieve me.

Let's get separated I can't handle and lead any more this life anymore, she added.

Gangu's husband replied that's one thing you will never get and never ask.

After we will separate what will I do where will I go, he added.

Gangu's life went on, day by day, as the years passed. Her children were growing up, and each year brought new problems and milestones. Despite the passage of time, the torment she experienced remained a constant in her life, nearly becoming an accepted part of her everyday existence. She endured her pain with calm courage, taking comfort in the pleasures of watching her children grow. Gangu's perseverance remained unwavering despite her difficult circumstances. She approached each day with a determined attitude, expressing an unwavering will to persevere for the sake of her family.

# CHAPTER TWENTY-FIVE

# Struggle to Earn a Livelihood

In 1978, the Factory Gangu was working when workers went on strike. The strike was between two unions. The factory had over 1000 workers. 400 hundred workers were on strike and the rest were at the factory. All the junior staff were involved in the union and were outside hence the were only senior staff there which included the executive and department head Gangu was the only woman working there during this strike. She wonderfully handles the office in an era of crisis. As employees were overburdened due to a lack of junior staff each of the existing employees was working beyond their duties.

Gangu also worked beyond her duty during this period she learnt to use fax machines.

Meanwhile the Managing Director and Boss would also join employees in doing small works.

Gangu would ask them to stay in the cabin.

You are making us nervous, she would say.

The strike carried on almost for 8 months. Meanwhile, they were stopping the people who were working inside the office. Some supervisors in the factory were even stabbed. As the situation was getting worse the company gave each employee a bodyguard. Gangu was also given a bodyguard who was an ExNavy officer. Their names are registered at a nearby police station for safety purposes. Day by day this situation was getting worse.

As the workers who were sitting on strike were not able to come inside the office, they started sending a group of people to create a disturbance while they were working.

They started attacking the cars of the staff who were presently working for the company therefore Gangu would go to the company by public bus. The bus stop was near the company and her bodyguard stayed near the bus stop.

As they came to know about this they started waiting at the bus stop. One day Gangu was getting off the bus and suddenly a group of people came near Gangu chasing her not to go to work.

Gangu bravely answers them who are you to stop me from going to work?

As soon as Gangu told them they started showing knives to Gangu to frighten her.

As Gangu saw the knife Gangu ran steadily.

They were following Gangu and the bodyguard was helpless about what to do. And Gangu's workplace was on the first floor. Gangu went to her side of the office building luckily she hid herself in another company's office.

They ran to the shelter-skelter in anger to fetch Gangu and threaten her. As the situation got cold Gangu went to the office as the management came to know about the incident and they were deeply upset and worried.

Meanwhile, there was a petrol pump where a boy from Gangu's community was working. They pressure that boy and ask him to explain to Gangu not to go to work. They even gave a warning that they would harm her kids. The poor boy came running to Gangu and told about them.

Don't come for work they are very dangerous your life will be in threat, Boy said to Gangu.

Don't worry I will manage, Gangu replied to the boy.

I will take care of myself, Gangu added.

Suddenly all of them came outside the building as Gangu was inside and started abusing her as they were speaking in Marathi Gangu could not understand what they were speaking.

Meanwhile, the Managing director's daughter was along with her.

She asked Gangu, do you understand Marathi?

Gangu said, No!

The managing director's daughter said, good whatever they are talking about doesn't make any sense to you. Be happy!

Meanwhile, Gangu was carrying on with turbulence as it was a question of herbread and butter. Well, it was the weekend Gangu gave a holiday to the maid. As normal she was frying chips for the children. Suddenly the gas went and she started using the stove of kerosene. Unfortunately, a tragedy took place while she was attaching the stove of the hot vessel which contained oil split over Gangu. The vessel fell on the thighs of Gangu due to which was severely scorched. Little Vishal was around her Gangu's motherhood arose. She just forgot her pain and tried to save Vishal away from the splited oil. While protecting him Gangu ends up getting her right hand burned deeply.

In immense pain, Gangu was thinking about how she would go to work and she was leading the office as well.

The next day Gangu called the boss and told the incident.

The boss asked, is it okay if he brings the file to home can you do it from there?

Gangu replied I will try.

Somehow Gangu managed with one hand as there was a lot of pending work remaining in the office. The boss was aware of the accident that took place with Gangu. As Gangu was a brave pillar all the colleagues were asking about Gangu to the boss.

The boss told them she was not keeping well, therefore she was not coming.

Not to visit her house as she will be well she will come back, he added.

Gangu's wound was deep it took her 3 to 6 weeks to recover. The thigh wounds were so deep that she had to approach a specialist. It was so bad that told her to get an artificial leg. When she started recovering Gangu started to go to work. Simultaneously after 8 months, the trade unions who were at the strikes lost the case and they were back to work. Meanwhile, they were so humiliated they would not raise their heads when seeing Gangu around. As usual, Gangu forgave them but she would taunt them some time that we were working well without you.

# CHAPTER TWENTY-SIX

# Years of Grief

Years were passing and there was no relief for the pain. Gangu was carrying on. Gangu has no purpose in life except to be a protective shell to her children. In the torture, he plans different ways for the mastermind to torture her. He threatens Gangu to come along with him for a movie. Otherwise, he would bash the children. To protect the children Gangu would go with him. He would take her along but he would vanish at the gate of the theater. He would buy many tickets together and sell them in black. However, Gangu would wait outside waiting for him at the theatre like a fool. After selling all the tickets he would take Gangu inside the theater and make her sit at the corner somewhere. While he would sit between the girls to whom he has sold the tickets.

Soon after having this behaviour, Gangu would refuse to go with him to watch a movie. But he would torture if you don't come I will bash your children. Gangu was helpless, she just didn't want her children to suffer.

When she was standing outside the cinema theatre a strange man came to Gangu and said, you are waiting for me, let's go and see the movie.

Gangu replied, go from here, I am waiting for my husband.

The man was so nasty he was trying to hold Gangu's hand.

Gangu just screamed and she saved herself from the horrifying incident which was about to happen.

Meanwhile, the husband came and didn't react to anything.

Gangu's husband was a monster. He didn't leave a single opportunity to put Gangu in pain. Gangu had a habit of organizing all the things required for tomorrow. She would iron the saree and keep the belongings ready in advance to be punctual at the job. Her husband would take the saree and throw it into the bucket of water in the bathroom. Gangu didn't react much because she didn't want to waste time. She would wear the another saree and go.

Whenever the Gangu's husband was not at home she would have a lovely time with her sons. They would smile in joy at the movement he would enter and their blossoming face would be turned pale. Gangu and Vikram were suffering a lot mentally the younger son Vishal was under the cover of both of them.

In 1981, Gangu's father started getting ill. He was hospitalized. As soon as Gangu heard about that she rushed to Madikeri. It was becoming quite difficult for them to stay alone at Madikeri. Gangu's mother was also getting sick now and managing the huge house was not that easy. They were searching for servants but they were not up to mark being trusted. Gangu was holding all the responsibility of daughter as well as mother hence she came back after a few times.

Meanwhile, Gangu's parents were unable to fetch a good servant. As a daughter, Gangu told them to come to Bombay and stay with her if they wanted.

She is also cautious that the Bombay lifestyle and Madikeri lifestyle a different between the moon and the sun. Before coming to Bombay come and stay one month to see if it works for you, Gangu told then.

Gangu's parents landed in Bombay with all their belongings. The lifestyle which Gangu has in Bombay is 360 degree different from the Madikeri . They would keep an eye on what Gangu was doing. They even try to rule Gangu. Gangu can't carry on as she had set a routine. Once in the evening, Gangu was talking with the lady who was staying downstairs for a few minutes. As soon as she went to her apartment, her mother stood at the door.

Gangu was puzzled. Gangu's mother said, where were you so long?

I saw you entering the colony at 7 o'clock and it's already 7:15, Gangu's mother added.

And she started scolding Gangu badly. Gangu just kept quiet out of respect. Gangu has a habit of not giving back answers.

Meanwhile, Gangu's elder son was watching.

He asked Gangu, why didn't you say anything to her?

Gangu said, if I give back answers today, tomorrow you will give back answers to me. It's disrespectful.

While Gangu's housemaid was so helpful and punctual. She would give the food as routine as set by Gangu. Once there was Gangu's uncle who was very kind and had affection towards her. He came to Bombay for his treatment. He was diagnosed with tongue cancer. As he came to know

Gangu was living in Bombay came to see Gangu's house.

Gangu told him, you will get tired climbing the stairs since my apartment doesn't have an elevator.

Uncle said, No, I will come.

With the deadly disease, he climbed and came to Gangu's house.

Gangu was delighted to see him. She offered the snacks to eat but unfortunately, due to disease, he couldn't take them.

Meanwhile, after a few days, he died. Gangu didn't come to know about this news but her father was aware of it. They didn't inform Gangu and went to see the dead body. Suddenly from somewhere Gangu came to know that her uncle was dead by the time she could reach to see the dead body it had already been transported to airport to be taken to her native place.

Gangu's parents' attitude was strange. They were no longer brothered for her. Once Gangu's mother saw what the nasty man was doing with her saree every day.

She told Gangu, You have mastered patience. I saw what he had done to your saree.

If it could be another girl he would create a conflict, Gangu's mother added.

While Gangu stayed quiet as she only knew what she was suffering. For almost one year her mother stayed with them and Gangu's mother decided to get back to Mysore. Gangu had done the packing and they left.

# CHAPTER TWENTY-SEVEN

# Battle for Freedom

Gangu had given up hope for a life free of torment. She grew to feel that facing adversity was simply part of her destiny. Despite the many hardships and discomfort she endured, she never complained. Instead, she smiled through it all, demonstrating her tenacity and courage. Gangu's resilience in the face of adversity was impressive. She continued to care for her children and do her obligations with unshakable commitment. Her silent perseverance and unwillingness to surrender to despair set a striking example of bravery and elegance under adversity.

As Vikram grew older, around the age of 13 or 14, he began to lose interest in his academics. Despite being an intellectually talented youngster, his grades were steadily declining. Gangu, who was like a friend to her kids, became more anxious. She kept asking him, "Why are you doing this?" Let me know if you have any difficulties." Gangu realised Vikram was not psychologically stable.

To assist him, she brought Vikram to a therapist, expecting that he would speak out if he was experiencing any difficulties. He refused to confide in the counsellor as well. Despite her best efforts, Vikram remained aloof, and his troubles continued to worry Gangu greatly. She saw that recognising and resolving the underlying cause of his anxiety was critical to his well-being and future success.

Gangu consoles him, you come up in your life build up yourself be independent.

She is there only for kids rest is of no use to her added

Likewise, time was going on and Vikram was almost 18 years of age in the year 1883.

Suddenly Vikram came to Gangu and gave an ultimatum.

Vikram said, 'Either you leave this man or I will kill this man'.

After killing I would be happy if I go to jail as the tortures of my mother's life have ended, he added

Gangu replied that which mother would be happy to see her child be in jail.

And when we can't give someone life we have no right to take someone's life, she added.

Gangu assured Vikram by saying, I will go for divorce.

Through one of the contacts, Gangu found a lawyer. He made an application to get him out of the house. Unfortunately, that petition was rejected. There was a lawyer in the colony who kept him to fight the case and called his father to send money to fight the case. After a few days, Gangu's husband's lawyer and her lawyer had a meetup they made a deal and he gave up the case.

Again Gangu was helpless don't know what to do. She went to the boss and disclosed the problem. Gangu was the most loyal employee of the organisation therefore she had always got the support. Boss took her to M.D.

Immediately he said don't worry I will arrange it for you.

He called a leading lawyer who was his family friend. The boss discloses the case to the lawyer on the phone.

The lawyer replied, that if I was handling a divorce case I would have fought without any fees but he suggested one of his criminal lawyers in government.

As soon as Gangu gathered all the information about the lawyer she went with the boss to the lawyer.

On meeting the lawyer he asked Gangu a couple of questions which Gangu answered truly. On hearing Gangu, he was furious and reacted your husband has no place to live in this world.

Then he said, look I am a criminal lawyer just finished him off.

I will give you a gun and you teach how to use and finish him. I will take you out of the prison, he added.

Gangu instantly replies that is something I will never do in my life just get me out of this.

Then the lawyer said, I don't handle divorce cases but I can help you I have someone.

Took them to another lawyer and made them meet the lawyer who handled divorce cases. The criminal lawyer gave the briefing of the case to the other lawyer. Upon understanding the cases he agreed to be Gangu's lawyer and told, He I was going to be fighting the case free of charge. Then the lawyer took all the papers. Gangu's case got started in the courtroom in 1983.

The cases carried for two years in court. Gangu would go bravely to the court hearing alone with the office driver secretly. Sometimes you do go with the managing director' daughter. Only the boss of the office knew about the case rest of the other employees were unaware. Like that, they have supported Gangu wonderfully in her toughest time. Dates after the date went for two years. The court hearing was challenging. The opposition lawyer would ask her the worst questions. Being brave and emotional at the same time Gangu burst out with tears in the courtroom.

On the other Gangu's lawyer was calm and cool down the situation would say, Is he having love with you? The way he asks the question.

Gangu would say, what are you saying nothing like that.

It seemed like a miracle had occurred in 1985. When Gangu's husband returned to India, in 1969. He promptly applied for immigration to return to the United Kingdom. His passport had been obtained in Aden, therefore he had to wait a for immigration approval. When it came through in 1985. This sequence of circumstances felt like a God-given blessing. He was pleased when he heard the news and expected Gangu to drop the case and accompany him to the United Kingdom. Meanwhile, Gangu silently observed what he was doing. Her husband completed all of the appropriate immigration paperwork and prepared to travel to the United Kingdom. He eventually left the country without informing the court

When his court day approached, he was noticeably absent. He migrated without notifying the court. Despite having court appearances scheduled two or three times, he never showed up, even though his lawyer would present on his behalf. This absence created quite a commotion since his choice to leave without informing the authorities complicated matters greatly. Gangu continued to witness the happenings from a distance. Her husband's surprise departure marked a dramatic shift in their tale, leaving many things unexplained while laying the groundwork for future occurrences.

Fortunately, Gangu's long-awaited day arrived after twenty-one years of relentless struggle. The court awarded her divorce in absentia.

The judge added, do you have any demand for divorce?

Gangu replied, 'No my lord! you have given me my freedom, that's enough for me. Thank you!'

The procedure was lengthy and required much documentation. Meanwhile, the court selected two counsellors from a reputable organisation to help her.

These two women interviewed Gangu, and after hearing her story, they were in tears.

They inquired, "How could you live with such a beast for twenty-one years? What happens if he murders you? "He is insane."

The counsellors provided a helping hand, giving Gangu their phone numbers and encouraging her to call them anytime she needed aid. They quickly notified the court in writing that Gangu needed a divorce without further delay. Their dread of her husband was obvious, as they continually stated that he was insane. However, Gangu felt certain that he would not murder her. She reasoned that if he killed her, he would struggle to exist because she had been handling all of the home costs in addition to his own.

A few days later, Gangu received the court order. This was the end of a long and difficult chapter in her life, clearing the way for a fresh start free of the shadows of her past. The counsellors' assistance and the completion of the divorce gave her a new feeling of optimism and empowerment.

Gangu's grief came to an end after twenty-one years. Gangu felt like he was on top of the world, with a wave of relaxation flowing over her like a cool wind. Her youngsters shared excitement, their faces beaming with happiness and their laughter resounding throughout the home. This was a watershed moment in their lives, an opportunity to go on without the weight of the past. The mood in their home was one of pleasure and hope, a dramatic contrast to the years of adversity they had experienced. With their newfound independence, they looked forward to a future full of promise and potential, ready to face whatever came their way.

*Do not let your daughter die living a dreadful life,*
*For what is not their fault, why are they punishing,*
*Dying each day from within,*
*It ok to be apart than crying each day from within,*
*Where is the society in sorrow?*
*Where is the society in violence?*
*Why do you teach your daughter to be suppressed rather than teaching*
*her to stand against,*
*It's high time to end those ugly marriages which are ruining your*
*daughter from within!!*

# CHAPTER TWENTY-EIGHT

# Divorce—The Beginning of an Era of Happiness!

Gangu's twenty-one years have been tarnished by unimaginable sorrow and brutality. Gangu has suffered enormous suffering and cruelty throughout her life, which appears to have left a scar on her existence. One would question where these folks were while she was struggling and fighting against the odds. The truth is that no one will defend you as long as you defend yourself. Only when you are at your lowest point do people begin to speak up, offering their opinions and judgements. Their comments frequently arrive too late, serving merely as a reminder of their absence when they were most needed.

The phrase "divorce" should not be viewed as ugly or humiliating; in fact, being separated is frequently a healthier and more powerful option than continuing in a relationship where one feels stifled or reduced. Gangu raises a profound issue for the world: why does society perceive circumstances in such binary terms, categorising them as either extremely awful or very excellent, with no opportunity for nuance? Gangu's decision to divorce was probably the finest one she ever made. Each day that followed was filled with new delight and excitement, especially because she could share these experiences with her children.

Gangu and her sons had a period of tremendous happiness and independence following then divorce, which she treasures and remembers warmly throughout her life. The suffocating presence of her ex-husband had been the only impediment to their shared happiness. When he was no longer in their lives, the veil of negativity lifted, allowing them to prosper and live a peaceful, joyful life together. Gangu's experience demonstrates that sometimes leaving a bad relationship is the key to opening a future full of opportunities and joy.

The divorce had a good influence on Gangu's family, particularly her children. Her eldest son's accomplishments surged to incredible heights, driving him forward at breakneck pace. Freed from the turmoil of his previous home, he focused his energies on academics and personal development, making incredible progress on his own, with no external aid.

Gangu's younger son, however, was only twelve years old at the time of separation. Gangu, being in charge of her income and no longer subject to her husband's financial tyranny, could finally afford tiny indulgences for their children. Every day after work, she'd bring home chocolate pastries, which gradually became a beloved habit. Goddess Lakshmi started staying with Gangu.

With his pure heart, the younger son excitedly waited at the door for Gangu's return. When he saw the cherished pastries, his face lit up with sheer excitement, and he danced with glee. These simple moments, full of laughter and enjoyment, represented the start of a new chapter for Gangu and her sons, one in which they could finally enjoy the freedom and joy that had previously been denied to them.

Gangu went to her hometown soon after her divorce was finalised, seeking consolation and a sense of belonging. Her parents reacted calmly and acceptably to her homecoming and the news of her separation. at the same time, Gangu changed her surname on all official documents, taking her father's surname to represent a new beginning. Gangu took solace in her parents' silent support as they accepted the transition with little fuss.

The trip turned out to be a lovely holiday for Gangu and her sons, providing much-needed relief from the turbulence they had been through. They spent a month immersed in the peaceful setting of her childhood home, reuniting with relatives and revelling in the comfort of old surroundings. The lads relished their new adventures, touring the countryside and building ties with family they had rarely seen.

Gangu easily resumed her professional routine once they returned to Mumbai. She did, however, return with a renewed sense of purpose and a stronger spirit. Her stay at her hometown had revived her, allowing her to tackle her tasks with renewed enthusiasm. Back in the city, Gangu and her sons began their lives with a new perspective, bolstered by the love and support they had received from relatives. This excursion represented the start of a new chapter, one full of optimism and the promise of brighter days to come.

It was a great pleasure for Gangu to come back home after work. Gangu and her children giggled and spent quality time together. Every weekend Gangu's party mode was on. Gangu with her sons would go for dinner and have a crazy weekend. At the same time, Gangu had developed an amazing bond with office colleagues. Gangu would enjoy working and the office was like a second home to her. After office hours they would go for dinner.

After twenty-one years of sadness and innumerable suffering, Gangu finally found peace. She had been through a terrible road filled with suffering and hardship, but she was now living life to the fullest. Each day offered fresh thrills and discoveries, minor pleasures that she had previously overlooked.

Gangu, no longer burdened by the weight of an oppressive marriage, began to see the world around her with new eyes. She appreciated the freedom to make decisions for herself and her children, focusing on the little things that brought them joy. She relished her boys' joy, their accomplishments, and the shared pleasures of ordinary life that had before felt so unreachable.

Her newfound serenity was more than simply the absence of suffering; it also included contentment and satisfaction. Gangu's tale evolved into one of perseverance and change, demonstrating the strength of the human spirit and the ability to find light even in the darkest of circumstances. Gangu, embracing her newfound independence, was finally living the life she had always desired: one of serenity, joy, and limitless possibilities.

*Gangu's family (Parents and children)*

*Gangu with her sons (Vikram & Vishal)*

# CHAPTER TWENTY-NINE

# Demise of Beloved Father and Mother

In the year 1986, Gangu got the news that her mother was not keeping well. Suddenly she went into a coma. On hearing the horrifying news Gangu rushed to Mysore. The kids of Gangu have grown up to be mature and caring. As Gangu decided to go to Mysore the elder son was worried for her as she had high blood pressure due to intense stress. Anything would happen to her. He was anxious that if she went there her health would turn terrifying. Therefore both the children came along with her.

Gangu went along with them to Mysore. Her mother was unconscious and was on death bed. Gangu went directly to the hospital to reach Mysore. Gangu's father had a lot of relatives in Mysore all were gathered at the hospital before Gangu would reach.

Gangu wouldn't hold her emotions out of affection Gangu loudly told mummy.

Guess what, in that condition, Gangu's mother opened her eyes and said you have come.

You are in this stage. I had to come, Gangu replied.

And again she closed her eyes which she never opened after that. Gangu's mother made her heavenly journey.

Gangu has never suffered such a tremendous loss before. The loss of her mother destroyed her world, filling her eyes with sorrow and breaking her heart. The anguish was tremendous; a profound sorrow wrapped her completely. Gangu viewed her mother as a source of strength and support, and losing her was like losing a piece of herself.

This horrible tragedy shocked and devastated Gangu's father. Gangu's parents had a deep link, and her father's anguish was evident, his heart heavy from the death of his lifetime partner. The home, which had previously been filled with Mysore's warmth and presence, now seemed painfully empty.

Gangu remained in Mysore for a few days following her mother's death, hoping to console and support her father while dealing with her grief. She attempted to keep herself together for his sake, even though she was deeply affected by her loss. Those days were filled with moments of shared grief, quiet introspection, and the consoling presence of relatives and friends who came to pay their respects and express their sympathy.

However, the strains of her life in Mumbai quickly drew her back. Her career and childrearing obligations could not be disregarded. Despite her heavy heart and lingering melancholy, Gangu realised she had to get back to her routine.

When Gangu returned to Mumbai, she attempted to focus on her career and her children's needs, hoping to regain some sense of normalcy despite the emotional upheaval. However, the death of her mother remained a profound sorrow in her heart, a reminder of the irreplaceable vacuum left in her life. During her sadness, Gangu found strength in her mother's memories, clinging onto the teachings and love that Mysore had bestowed and using them as a guide to navigate the tough days ahead.

Gangu realised her father was saddened when she departed. He had thought Gangu would stay with him forever. Despite this, Gangu called her father every day to see how he was doing. He first seemed to appreciate her care, but as time passed, he became increasingly frustrated by her constant calls.

One day, he ordered Gangu, "Stop phoning me every day. I'm not a child."

However, a daughter's heart is not easily broken. Gangu continued to call, despite her father's displeasure and rants. Despite his complaints, she felt driven to guarantee his well-being.

Meanwhile, Gangu learned that a couple had attempted to integrate themselves into her father's life, creating a sense of family for him. Her father had also donated several of her mother's sarees and valuables to them. Gangu was aware of some of the events in her father's life, while others were unknown to her. Despite the distance and strain, Gangu remained alert and worried, attempting to combine her obligations in Mumbai with her steadfast devotion to her father.

In 1987 the Gangu's father started falling sick and something was fishy as well. All the relatives were warning Gangu that something was cooking.

When we go to your father's house he doesn't open the door, they told Gangu.

Gangu was puzzled as she couldn't go to Mysore now and then.

Finally, one day Gangu called her father and told I can sense Papa you are not keeping well shall I come to Mysore.

Why! You don't have to come to see, Gangu's father replied with a harsh tone.

Soon after a few days, Gangu's father started praising that couple. Narrating to Gangu they are very good and helpful. Gangu just kept on listening. On one final day, Gangu's father told Gangu that I was allowing them to stay at our house. On hearing this Gangu's blood was boiling.

Gangu told her father, before they shift to your place she want to meet him once.

Then do whatever he want to do, Gangu added.

As soon as Gangu reached her father's house the couple was already at home. They were saying, we will change the decoration of the house and so on.

Meanwhile, Gangu's father was not at all happy to see her. He was in miserable condition. His health was deteriorating. He was not able to move and has become skinny. He was having severe jaundice.

On seeing her father Gangu asked him with affection and care, what have you done to yourself?

Gangu's father became increasingly apathetic to her, expressing more care for the couple he had adopted as his "son" and financial benefactors. His efforts included supporting their endeavours and transferring property titles into their names, which contrasted sharply with his indifference to Gangu's wellbeing. This shift in his priorities greatly affected Gangu, emphasising the emotional gap that had grown between them.

Despite feeling disregarded, Gangu upheld her dignity and obligations. She persevered during this difficult era, aided by her extended family and friends in Mumbai, whose unwavering allegiance brought solace despite the chaos. While grappling with her father's favouritism towards the couple, Gangu found strength in her ideals and convictions, vowing to uphold them regardless of the situation.

The next day, Gangu found herself driving her father to the hospital and ensuring that he was hospitalised quickly. It was a time of urgency and anxiety, as his health had taken a turn that required medical treatment. Amidst this urgent scenario, the couple approached Gangu with questions about moving it to their house.

Faced with the couple's continuous questions, Gangu stated firmly, "Papa is currently in the hospital." I'm not sure what he talked with you. Please do not make any move till he gets home. Her statements had a tone of authority and protection, showing her intention to defend her father's interests and prevent rash judgements in his absence.

Throughout this difficult time, Gangu juggled the duties of handling her father's health problems with the complex dynamics of the young couple. Despite external pressures and uncertainty, she stayed committed to helping her father and upholding his desires. This episode highlighted Gangu's fortitude and dedication to her father's well-being, despite the familial conflicts and competing interests at play.

Each day Gangu's father was not showing a any sign of improvement each day his health was getting worse. He stayed in the hospital for fifteen days.

Doctors gave up and told Gangu, there was no hope for life. Unfortunately, Gangu's father died. And Gangu had to endure the pain of losing again. This time little Vishal was there with her. Both the children loved the Gangu unconditionally. Meanwhile, all the other relatives were there at the hospital. Gangu's paternal uncle and aunt made all the arrangements for the funeral.

Soon after returning from the funeral one of the cousins called Gangu asked, What about this couple? I have heard they asked father to have made a will in their name.

The couple just thought they would bully her and take away all the things as Gangu was alone.

Gangu's cousin suggested, just searching the papers.

Will come tomorrow, Gangu's cousin added.

Meanwhile, the couple stayed at Gangu's home. Gangu observed they were searching for something. At the same time, Gangu searches for papers but can't found. When the couple saw that Gangu had strong support from relatives and friends they started getting cold feet. Especially cousins gave her good support.

The next day, Uncle and Gangu's cousins came for a visit. Gangu informed them that she had not yet located the key document they were looking for. Uncle cautioned her, "Be careful about what the entire community is saying about them." Their motives are not good. But remember, Gangu, that we are on your side."

Numerous disagreements have erupted over the property, causing discontent and stress. Gangu, however, was able to handle the tumult thanks to the community's unshakable support and Uncle's persistent advice. Uncle, using his power and contacts, organised the sale of the property, resolving the conflicts in a fairly short amount of time. Given the situation's intricacy, the conclusion was quick, almost miraculous.

With the problem resolved, Gangu returned to Bombay, their minds at peace and spirits elevated. Her family and community's support had helped her overcome the hurdles, cementing the links of trust and solidarity. Gangu felt a newfound feeling of optimism and strength, ready to confront whatever came next with the same tenacity and courage.

# CHAPTER THIRTY

# Achievement to New Heights—-Business

The life of Gangu was going smoothly with joys and giggles. At the same time, her children were growing and achieving. Gangu gave a new sky to her dream and she started travelling from the year 1988. She would work hard and save money for travelling. Each year she had international trips.

Meanwhile, the elder son of Gangu secured a job all by his dedication and hard work in the year 1989. Gangu was quite impressed with him and always had good wishes. While the younger son was pursuing microbiology. On the other hand, Gangu was doing solo trips as her sons have grown up. She had kept the maid for cooking and other household chores.

By 1993 she had explored countries—Hong Kong, Denmark, Thailand and Dubai. She would work hard for eleven months and spend savings on travelling. Likewise, she was developing other sources of income such as trading stock. She would take the calculative risk of not investing money not more than ten thousand. Due to this, she had made a significant amount of profit.

However, the days were going on and with experience, Gangu got expertise in almost every operational unit of the office. She was almost aware of everything such as marketing, sales, finance and so on. Gangu was losing interest in being someone's employee. It has been almost 25 years since Gangu worked in different sectors. Slowly and gradually her interest turned to founding a business.

Meanwhile, there was another employee who was with the same mindset. He was in the sales department. He narrated the idea and Gangu agreed with him. Starting a business was not a piece of cake. Every penny gets into building the business. luckily Gangu had funds that she had received after the death of her father.

On the other hand, Vikram progressed to a higher peak in a short period. He was posted to Germany, Frankfurt. He was the youngest foreign manager of his company. He was just in his 20s. It was a joyful environment all around Gangu, delighted and proud. On the other hand that company organised a huge party to celebrate the youngest manager.

Vishal was quite emotional and upset after hearing the posting of his brother.

He was very close to Vikram the most.

Vishal told Gangu, why Aana ( *brother*) has to go so far.

He can work here.

Gangu explained to Vishal, no dear Aana has to grow and has to come up in life.

Meanwhile, Vishal was in the final year of microbiology. Gangu and Vikram were planning for Vishal to send him to Australia for further studies.

Gangu was aggressively working to establish a business. Her Partner suggested two places: Mysore and Bangalore. Gangu had the knowledge of both places and Mysore was her place of childhood holiday on the other hand Bangalore was expensive due to MNCs. Gangu had confidence in Mysore since she had seen it more closely.

Gangu started to search for a place in Mysore. She went to the industrial area but couldn't find any. They were highly corrupt. Finally one of her cousins of Gangu came to know that she was fetching a business place and he helped her to buy the place. Since Gangu came from Bombay to buy the place they were asking double the price of land to Gangu. Somehow Gangu managed to buy the land. The land was worth paying high.

Fortunately, Gangu started with all the legal documents to start a business. It took many months to get a few papers signed as the government's employees were all corrupt. Somehow Gangu managed but it was very tough. It was a very different experience for Gangu. After doing all that documentation the struggle was to get the electricity and water facility.

Gangu was hard-working; she was doing the job as well as establishing that business. On weekends she could take the night flight to Mysore to keep the check of how the business is working. Gangu went up and down until the business was established. Although Vikram was working Gangu was only running the house even if he was offering. Gangu never interfered with what he was doing with money and investing. Finally, construction was done and Fortunately, the production units started in mid-1993.

For Gangu and her business partner, the fruits of their labour were finally starting to sprout. Gangu handled the vital supply chain side of their company while her partner handled the machinery, manufacturing, and raw materials. They celebrated the opening of their production facility at the end of 1993, following months of intense work. It was an important turning point that represented the fruition of their vision and tenacity. Vishal, who was instrumental in their trip, eagerly took part in the event. Vikram, whose out-of-town obligations prevented him from being present, was nevertheless present in spirit and played a crucial role in their accomplishment. The occasion, which marked the start of a bright new phase in their entrepreneurial adventure, was a monument to their combined grit and will.

Gangu and her business partner took a calculated risk when the production unit started up, choosing to meet orders over keeping big stocks in a cutthroat industry. The company's efficient and quick operations to consumer needs helped it stand out from its many competitors.

Even though the company was operating smoothly, Gangu made a big decision: she decided to quit its job. She gave it much thought and put her reasons for leaving in writing when she filed her resignation. Despite being comprehensible, this action demoralised her coworkers and the management group. Nonetheless, they managed all the required procedures with professionalism and effectiveness, demonstrating the respect and commitment to each other that had defined Gangu's time working for the organisation.

Gangu's departure from the position represented a change in focus towards happiness and maybe a well-earned break after years of hard work. While it signalled the end of an era, it also created new opportunities and experiences outside of the corporate world.

Soon after she resigned, Gangu worked full-time for her company and brought the company to new heights. Soon after a few days of working full-time for the company she invested in buying a plot in Mysore. She built the bungalow on that plot which took a lot of time to get built. Gangu gave a personal touch to the bungalow bringing different kinds of decorations from all over the world. The rare creative masterpiece was bought for Italy and Germany. Little bit and piece arranging Gangu made an elegant bungalow.

Likewise, progress to be a businesswoman. She started multiple businesses after a partnership business. Proprietorship, small trading company supplying plastic pouches, floriculture company exporting flowers.

International differences were an unforeseen obstacle to Gangu's ambitious floriculture plan, preventing her from launching the enterprise she had envisaged for the area she had invested in. Not to be disheartened by this setback, Gangu cleverly turned around. With passion and effort, she transformed the property into a lively farm, growing a wide range of fruits and flowers. Gangu made a more selfless decision to market her goods rather than sell it for a profit. She set out on a quest to provide happiness and plenty to her hometown of Mysore. Every harvest season turned into a festival as she gave her fruits and flowers to friends, neighbours, and complete strangers.

Many said Gangu could sell her abundant harvest and make good money, but she was happiest when she was helping others. More satisfying to her than any financial benefit were the smiles and appreciation she received in return. Gangu saw farming as a work of love, a means of nurturing both her land and the spirits of people around her.

Her choice to put giving above profit was a perfect example of her individuality and her steadfast dedication to bringing joy via small deeds of kindness.

# CHAPTER THIRTY-ONE

# Tragedy in the City– Bombing

Suddenly in the year 1993,while Gangu was working still in the office there was a series of massive bomb explosions in Bombay. As usual, Gangu was at work as well as Vikram was at work. While Vishal was in college. Gangu was working suddenly Gangu's boss gave the news that there was a bomb explosion at the stock exchange.

When Gangu learned of the explosion at the stock exchange, she was instantly frozen. Vishal's fear was heightened by the fact that his college was located near the stock exchange. She started to tremble violently, her mind racing with worries about Vishal's safety in the middle of all the chaos going on around them.

By no thought, it just came to Gangu's mouth that it wouldn't stop there only there would be more bombs to come. Gangu just ran to her cabin wondering what to do now and how to contact her sons. Immediately after a few minutes Gangu's Boss came and said there was an explosion in the Air India building. On the other hand, Vikram's office was close to Air India and Gangu's office was located at Worli.

Gangu was more tense about her sons instead of her. It was all broadcasted on the television about Bombay City; many people were dying and as well as getting injured. Gangu needed help to contact them. Gangu was getting numb. Soon after the telephone line froze due to Bombay so they couldn't pass the message ahead. Luckily Gangu's managing director line was working as they have a direct connection.

Gangu was the only woman executive in the office. The Managing director was aware that Gangu's son was working near the Air India building. He just sensed Gangu's situation.

As soon as he came to know his line was working he came running to Gangu and asked her to connect the call to her sons. Soon everybody from the office came running to the cabin of Gangu. While Gangu was there in great shock she was not in condition to speak a word. All of them were asking for the contact numbers of her sons since Gangu was frozen they managed to get their contact numbers from directories.

Meanwhile, the canteen man bought a coffee for a Gangu. Soon after drinking the coffee, she was a bit better. Everyone pulled her from the chair and took her to the managing directors' cabin. While at the same time, everybody was searching for their numbers. Finally, they got the number and the bell rang.

Luckily it was Vikram on the call. Listening to Vikram's voice Gangu just got some relief.

Vikram told Gangu, the situation here is not good. I can see the Air India building glasses are falling.

Gangu just suggested that he stay in office only. Till the situation cools down.

Vikram how do we call Vishal, Gangu added.

Meanwhile, Vikram asked Gangu to wait for a minute as his other line was ringing.

Gangu was holding on to the call while on the other line, it was Vishal.

Vishal was asking for an update from Vikram about how he is.

Vikram asked him and suggested he stay where he was.

Vishal added, how do we connect to our mother?

Vikram informs Vishal that Mama is on another line.

Vikram gave the update about Vishal to Gangu as well.

Gangu told Vikram to stay in the office while she told Vishal to stay in college only. As there was continuous bombing everywhere.

She informed them that she was also there in the office.

Gangu was relieved and was at peace after having a conversation with her son. She couldn't stop thanking the Managing director.

The Managing director was so supportive and kind that he told Gangu I can understand how a mother feels.

Now you get to relax, he added.

Everyone was there in the office only as it was risky to move out. Finally, around 4:30 PM it stopped bombing and everyone started moving. Gangu saw the bloodshed all over the streets. Fortunately, Gangu reached home by 6 o'clock. Her maid as tensed as Gangu has not reached home. Her maid was relieved after seeing her. While the sons were at home by 8 p.m.

Life returned to its normal rhythm the next day as if nothing had occurred. Mumbaikars' tenacious spirit was seen once more, displaying their unflinching bravery in the face of difficulty. People resumed their everyday activities with a resolve and tenacity that typified their city, notwithstanding the upheaval of the day before.

# Shock of the Biggest Loss—Vishal

Soon after the posting in Germany, Vikram gave the Gangu trip to Europe. As Gangu was mad about travelling she couldn't wait, she just accepted the gift with an open heart. But before going for the trip Gangu went to Germany to meet Vikram. Gangu was delighted seeing the achievement Vikram had made.

There she went on a trip to Europe. Gangu reached Italy safely. Due to jetlag, she was extremely tired. Suddenly it was around 4:30 AM Gangu woke up from a horrifying dream. She saw in the dream one of her sons was wrapped in a white cloth but which son was he she couldn't figure out. Her heart was pumping badly. She was all sweaty due to fear. Gangu was just frozen, not aware of what to do it was July 28.

She just rushed to the post office brought the telephone card and called Vikram. He was out of the station on duty so she called Vishal. As soon as he picked told Gangu,' I love you, mama'

Gangu becomes more emotional.

She asked him to connect to Vikram and get an update on his brother. Since connecting the call was a difficult task.

Vishal gave the update to Gangu that Vikram is fine by that time it was evening.

Meanwhile, Gangu didn't at all enjoy the trip. The dream was recurring again and again in her mind. Again the same night Gangu had the dreadful dream reoeated. She was sure is 29th july something would happen to one of the children. She will lose one of her sons. Gangu carried on with the trip and suddenly she lost her heartbeat and miraculously immediately came back. There was intense pain in the chest. Unfortunately, Gangu couldn't understand what was happening and went back to the hotel and took some rest.

Somehow Gangu carried on and came back to Germany to Vikram. In Germany, she had a heart attack at night. She didn't tell Vikram anything and traveled to Bombay. While Vishal was there at home, delighted to see her. She told him that she is not well and want to see a doctor. He said he will take her. Vishal had a birthday party in the evening of one of his friends, therefore he told Gangu, I will be late tonight. And Vishal left for the party. Meanwhile, Gangu was tired and didn't realise when she went to sleep.

Suddenly it was around 2 AM Gangu's telephone rang loudly. Gangu was puzzled as to who was there at the call so late.

Gangu picked the call. It was from the police station.

The policeman said Am I speaking to Vishal's family member?

Gangu replied, Yes!

Your child has met with an accident, the policeman said.

Gangu asked, Would you please give the telephone to him?

The policeman said, Have some courage, Be courageous dont come alone your child is no more.

As soon as she heard the news she went into great shock. She just ran towards his bedroom to check. Unfortunately, he was not there. Gangu was not in the state to talk to anyone. But she had to be brave enough as there was no one with her. Gangu just called the business partner and went with him to the police station. As soon as she reached the police station she verified the body was Vishal. Right from childhood Gangu took two times more care of Vishal than Vikram. He would fall sick very offen. Gangu's world just froze.

The policeman told Gangu to took the body to postmortem by themselves since their procedure will take time.

Listening to Policeman Gangu take the body to postmortem with a heavy heart.

The struggle she had upbringing was just lying in front of her. The postmortem generally takes place at a government hospital. Meanwhile, many community people were staying in Bombay as soon as they got the news they came for help. Gangu wanted to get the body that day itself so she requested the doctor.

The doctor was so cruel he asked for eight thousand to release the body.

As the community people gathered they heard the doctor, How can you say this? She has been raising her children with utmost difficulty. Who cares about pain and difficulties, everything is the game of money.

Gangu raised her voice and said he had to collect the money he must have promised his wife while coming here. He was butcher not a doctor.

Meanwhile, trying to connect Vikram as he kept on travelling and somehow community people connected him. Vikram was in Frankfurt. It was the longest flight of Vikram of his life. Time Finally, Vikram landed and did all the last rituals of Vishal. All the smiles of Gangu's family just disappeared. Both Vikram and Gangu were in extreme pain and sorrow.

*How can you say bye when your mother is alive,*
*You told me that you love me why are you saying goodbye,*
*Your mother's heartbeat has stopped seeing you going,*
*Comeback again your mother wants to see you smile,*
*I know you will not come back you love to play hide and seek,*
*Your mother gave up today you are winner,*

Gangu couldn't accept the fact that her son was gone. Gangu's health was badly affected.

Before going to Germany Vikram took Gangu for a check-up. Vikram took her to hospital. Only the thing is that Gangu requested him to take her for a full body checkup as Gangu just thought something major was happening inside her. All the tests were taking place one after the other. First, she gave a blood sample then she went for an ECG.

As soon as the ECG was done the consultant doctor told Gangu, I don't want to talk to you.

Is there any responsible person with you, she added.

Gangu replied, 'Yes! My son'.

The doctor told Gangu to call him.

Vikram came inside the cabin and the doctor said, Do you know she had a major heart attack?

And she carried on like this. I am just wondering how she is carrying on and walking, The doctor added.

Vikram told the doctor Before you make any judgement. I have a story. He narrated the entire incident of Vishal's death.

As soon as the doctor heard about the incident she burst out crying .

And told Gangu, I apologise I was rude to you.

She managed all the processes by herself for Gangu. She suggested if you go by the process it will take a long time. Her main artery was blocked 99.8 per cent. Immediate Bypass surgery was needed. Gangu knew Vikram had to go back to Germany for his commitments.

Gangu told the doctor, Give me some tablets I will manage. My son has work. He will arrange it and come back.

It was risky but Gangu stayed on tablets for a few days. It was very difficult for Gnagu she was completely on bed rest. Vikram was back after a month. He took the appointment for the best cardiologist in the City. And Gangu was admitted for the operation. After the surgery, Gangu became conscious after 36 hours. Soon after the operation, there were other complications the fluid got inside the lungs. Due to this, she stayed at I.C.U. for nearly 15 days. It was so bad that they were another patient with the same problem who had just died.

Vikram took the utmost care of Gangu staying right outside the I.C.U there was a seat Vikram would sleep there. Fortunately, doctors pumped the fluid from the lungs and it was better. Thankfully Gangu's health was improving and she was shifted to the private ward. After twenty-one days she was given the discharge. But Gangu had to visit the hospital now and then for check-ups to see fluid reduces in the lung.

During this time, Vikram suffered one side was the death of his dearest brother while on the other side, his mother was fighting for her life. Luckily Gangu was better physically but she died from inside. She had lost interest in living it took a year for Gangu to come out of dismissing of son.

Meanwhile, Vikram went to Germany and came back again but there was no improvement in Gangu's behaviour. He was just disturbed by seeing Gangu. Gangu has never been like this before, even at the demise of her parents.

Gangu asked Vikram to go to Germany as there were many good friends in the colony who were like a family to her. And Vikram went Gangu was carried on alone. With her friend's support.

One day Vikram lost his patience and asked Gangu, Mom, I gave you enough time to grieve.

You are crying so much for dead but you are not even thinking of the one who is alive, who wants you he added.

Listening to Vikram's words, just gave Gangu a sudden shock.

Gangu hugged him and said I am going to be living for you my son. I will not think of dead now.

From that day Gangu got a new purpose for life. Slowly she started coming back to normal. Vikram teaches Gangu how to concentrate on life and inspires her each day. She started focusing on her focusing on business and her son.

# CHAPTER THIRTY-THREE

# Hope for Life Again

Slowly and gradually Gangu started coping in life. Her factory was in Mysore and her office was in Bombay. Gangu would travel from Bombay to Mysore often. At the same time, Vikram was in Germany and was in constant touch with Gangu. Health-wise Gangu was struggling but was better than before.

Gangu decided after a few days to rent a home in Mysore because she was going there regularly. The property, located in a quiet, attractive suburb, gave her a feeling of security and a place to call home while she travelled. As word spread among her family and the local community that Gangu was in Mysore, many people came to see her to express condolences. Gangu gradually regained her life, thanks to the support of her loving son. She allowed herself to grieve while also embracing the times of joy and peace.

Gangu's unbreakable attitude drove her to restart her travels in 1995. She headed off again to see the world, motivated by her lifelong desire to learn about new places and cultures. This newfound spirit of adventure represented a key turning point in her life. Each journey she took helped her recover and rekindle her passion for life.

Gangu's extensive travels have led her to around 65 countries, each adding to her wealth of experiences and fond memories. Countries which Gangu travelled are Germany, Romania, Sweden, Serbia, Greece, Turkey, Egypt, Denmark, Switzerland, South Africa, Lebanon, Morocco, Zambia, Ethiopia, Kenya, Argentina, Brazil, Peru, Amazon, Chilli, Australia, New Zealand, Hong Kong, UAE, Myanmar, Jordan, Thailand, Indonesia, Singapore, Vietnam, Sri Lanka, Malaysia, Syria, China, Israel, Belgium, Hungary, Netherland, Luxembourg, Norway, UK, Armenia, France, Poland, Portugal, Austria, Italy, Spain.

When Gangu decided to embark on another journey, Vikram conveyed his concerns about her health . Gangu soothed Vikram about his fears but was astonished when he insisted on accompanying her on the trip 1995 first trip after Vishal's dead.

Although Gangu was used to travelling alone, she welcomed Vikram's companionship with open arms. Their vacation to Spain was especially meaningful because it coincided with Vikram's 30th birthday. Gangu threw a surprise party to commemorate, creating a welcoming and joyous environment. They met with both friends and locals, exchanging tales, laughing, and the joy of being together in a distant environment.

The journey not only confirmed their love and friendship, but it also served as a reminder of the value of collecting moments of joy and connection, no matter what the circumstances. It was an adventure filled with love, laughter, and a shared appreciation for life's beauty, making Vikram's birthday celebration in Spain a treasured experience for both of them.Then they went to Spain.

Vikram being an emotional and mama's boy decided to quit the job and join the partner of Gangu in Bombay.

Gangu explains with affection that you will not like to work with him.

You are well settled in Germany, don't worry about me. I have my friend as well.

I will visit you every three months, Gangu added.

Vikram refused all and said it was at fault because of him they lost Vishal.

Anyway, he resigned from the job and came back to India. He started working with Gangu's business partner. As predicted before by Gangu Vikram was not able to settle himself with him.

Gangu told Vikram, 'I know that man since I invested money. I am with him'.

Gangu suggested Vikram to ask his company to take him back.

Fortunately, his company welcomed him back with open arms and a hearty hug. This time, in 1996, he was assigned to London, a place that offered fresh prospects and experiences. Meanwhile, Gangu continued her adventures, going throughout the world and visiting many Indian states with her distinctive love for life. Despite the distance, their relationship remained strong, and Gangu would occasionally go to London to see Vikram, taking advantage of every chance to spend time together. These visits were full of delight and excitement as they explored the colourful country together and made lasting memories. Despite their hectic schedules and the distance between them, they always found a way to keep in touch, their love and bonding becoming stronger.

Gangu once flew to London on Mother's Day, which occurred to be a fortunate coincidence. Vikram, to whom Gangu meant everything, viewed this as an ideal chance to make the day particularly memorable for her. He created a surprise that would live in Gangu's mind forever.

On that momentous day, Vikram gave Gangu a stunning bouquet. This wasn't just any bouquet; it was a massive arrangement of fresh, brilliant red roses that had been meticulously selected to match Gangu's height exactly. The bouquet's sheer size and beauty were breathtaking, and Gangu was left speechless, stuck in a state of complete astonishment and happiness.

However, Vikram's kindness did not stop there. Along with the magnificent flower, he sent Gangu her favourite scent and a selection of fine chocolates. Perfumes were Gangu's ultimate weakness; she was obsessed with them. Her collection was large and varied, with each bottle reflecting a distinct tale or memory. Adding a new scent to her collection, particularly one picked with such care by Vikram, was a moving gift.

He chose a very excellent perfume because he knew how much she liked wonderful fragrances. Each time Gangu wore it, she was reminded of Vikram's sincere surprise and great devotion to her. The chocolates were also a nice touch to brighten up the day.

Gangu's love of scents was well-known to those around her. She was completely hooked on them, constantly looking for new and distinctive perfumes to add to her already amazing collection. Her eyes would light up with delight anytime she discovered a new perfume, and this present from Vikram was no exception. It demonstrated his grasp of her passions and interests, as well as his effort to make her feel valued.

Gangu recalls Mother's Day in London as one of the most memorable days of her life. The great gestures, thoughtful presents, and affection that Vikram put into every detail made her feel extremely special.

Similarly, as the days passed, Vikram never missed an opportunity to make her feel like she was on top of the world. He always found a way to make her day better, whether by thoughtful gestures, sweet words, or simply being there for her when she needed it. His persistent efforts and genuine concern made every minute they spent together exceptional and unforgettable, resulting in a profound friendship that grew deeper each day.

In 2003 Vikram decided to come back to India into a corporate office. Gangu and Vikram are living together. As usual, Gangu would frequently travel for business to Mysore. Meanwhile, Vikram was doing well and he was promoted to the Chief Operating Officer of one section. His company was going through a crisis therefore his company was winding up. Vikram worked with new management for a sometime but he couldn't love working with them. At the same time, he heard that his previous company had started in between operational activities. He had joined them again and they welcomed him with open arms in the year 2006. Hardly ten days he would stay in Bombay rest all days he was out of station. The great thing was that Vikram loved his profession.

# CHAPTER THIRTY-FOUR

# Death of Elder Son—-Vikram

Vikram and Gangu had an unusual and amazing bond. For Gangu, Vikram was more than
a crucial part of her life; he was the reason she existed. Her days focused on his happiness and well-being, after the death of Vishal. Vikram, on his part, cared profoundly about Gangu. He respected her devotion, dedication, and unlimited love for him. Their relationship was a lovely mix of friendship and commitment, and each day was a celebration of their special link. Vikram's presence brightened Gangu's life, and they worked together to weave treasured memories.

Gangu always says I am blessed to have a son like Vikram. Vikram always made Gangu proud. He nurtures Gangu with love and affection. He was an ideal son and every son would be like him, Gangu narrated. Wherever Gangu was in pain he came to Gangu as a medicine while Gangu's happiness was his happiness. Gangu called him her Sharvan Kumar who was totally devoted to mother.

Gangu, with her deep passion for travel, has visited about half of the world. Her friends and family were fully aware of her desire to see new locations and learn about diverse cultures. One evening, as Gangu and Vikram were sitting together and enjoying a calm time, Vikram took up a globe from the table nearby. With a cheerful smile, he turned to Gangu and asked, "Why don't you put your finger on the country you want to visit next?"

Gangu's eyes lit up with joy at the proposal. She stretched out and slowly spun the globe, watching as the countries blended into a bright swirl. After a few reflective seconds, she stopped the globe with her finger and checked to see where it had fallen. The suspense in the air was great, as Vikram leaned in to see which place had piqued her thirterest this time.

The simple yet profound process of selecting a new trip location drew them closer together, allowing them to share their aspirations for future journeys. This modest, spontaneous act demonstrated their relationship and shared passion for discovery and travel.

Come Mom I will arrange a trip to that country, Vikram said.

Whenever he would know that Gangu wanted something he would arrange that thing on that day itself. Nobody could beat Vikram in giving gifts. Once there was an advertisement for an elegant watch specially designed for Mother's Day. He brought that watch for Gangu and made her feel special. She is wearing that watch even today.

Gangu would ask him, why do you buy such expensive gifts for me, Raja?

Out of affection, he would say, Anything for my dearest mother.

He was the most obedient youngster, constantly adhering to the rules and showing respect. He demonstrated exceptional maturity from a young age, never generating any issues as he grew older. His calm and temperament distinguished him, he handled problems with maturity. His generosity and insightful remarks provided Gangu with comfort and support. He regularly showed compassion and empathy, whether by listening to others or simply being present when they needed it.

Gangu would say to him, why are you so close to me?

Vikram replied, Mama my umbilical cord is not cut therefore I am attached to you.

Gangu giggled and said, shameless child!

Travelling was part of his job whenever he was to come back to India and the driver would go to pick him up from the airport. The first thing he would ask was how the mother is. Wherever Ganga used to travel he would call her and stay connected wherever they were.

Time was flying Gangu was getting older. Throughout Her life, Gangu worked hard and provided for her children. As Gangu turned 60 years of age.

Vikram asked Gangu to stop working and enjoy the fruit of life.

I am here for you. Let me provide you, Vikram added.

But Gangu never listens to him and she continued working till the age of 70. At that time she didn't want to but due to her health condition, she had to. Vikram was Gangu's partner in happiness and sorrow. Her purpose in life.

Meanwhile, Gangu sold the bungalow and farm of Mysore. But sometimes she would go to relatives' functions such as weddings.

Sometimes Vikram would accompany her while sometimes Gangu would go alone.

Once it so happens there was the wedding at Mysore. Gangu was invited to the wedding. Luckily Vikram was in Mumbai this time. He joined Gangu and went to a wedding. The wedding was a colourful event, complete with colourful decor, upbeat music, and the pleasant companionship of family and friends. Vikram's pleasure at the event was extraordinary, and Gangu watched with great delight as her son revelled in the festivities. He took part in all of the rites, laughed heartily with relatives, and danced with a zest for life that radiated throughout the venue.

Gangu had never seen her child so joyful before. His sparkling laugh and the pure delight in his eyes filled her heart with pride and affection. It was as if all of his troubles had vanished, and he was living in the present with complete joy. Perhaps this happy involvement was even more painful because they had no idea it was Vikram's final meeting. His joyful presence at the wedding will live on in Gangu's heart forever. The sight of him so alive and happy became a treasured memory, representing the lively spirit and love he brought into their lives. The way Vikram enjoyed the wedding was next level. Gangu had never seen her child this happy before. Maybe because he was attending the last gathering of his life.

As they came back to Mumbai the microwave was not working. Vikram was about to go on a trip with his friend to Thailand. As Vikram came to know the microwave was not working he went to get the microwave from the shop. However, the brand which Gangu was using was not available at that time.

Gangu told Vikram, you change it when you come back, you buy for me.

Vikram replied, No! I can't leave my mother like that and go.

Vikram went to the warehouse and, after an extensive search, discovered the same microwave that Gangu had been using. He understood how much she cherished that specific model, with its familiar features and dependable performance. After securing the microwave, he returned, pleased to have discovered something that would provide her with comfort and constancy.

It was a Diwali vacation Vikram holiday mode was on it was the year 2019. He plans to go on a vacation with his friend. He went to Phuket for the trip. Gangu and Vikram were constantly in touch soon after reaching there Vikram called Gangu. It was not a long trip Vikram just for 3 to 4 days. It was one of the wishes of Vikram to do parasailing, luckily he had fulfilled his dream the same afternoon before catching the flight. Vikram was having his friend, friend's wife and son on the trip.

His friend was asking Vikram to pack up as they were having a flight in the evening.

Vikram told them from tomorrow onwards it would be just Work! Work! Work! Give me some 10 minutes, let me do the last swim and come back.

You go to the hotel I'll come back, He added.

Vikram's friend went to the hotel. It was more than 30 minutes but Vikram did not come. Vikram's friend was wondering where he was as they were getting late.

Vikram's friend's son said, Wait I'll go and see where the uncle is.

As soon as he reached near the beach they were trying to revive Vikram. The coast guard was there near. Vikram was still breathing therefore he shifted to hospital. Hospital people tried their best to revive him but they were unable to. And suddenly Vikram left the world giving the shock to near dear ones.

The next day, Vikram was expeated anytime, Gangu was quickly placing the breakfast table. It was the doorbell ringing. Upon opening the door, she found herself surrounded by a mournful group of Vikram's friends and colleagues who had made the trip to home.

Gangu could sense the seriousness on their faces and the weight of their silences. When they eventually revealed the devastating news of Vikram's passing, Gangu felt everything around her fall apart. Pale and numb, she stood there, unable to process the full scope of the loss. She had a tremendous jolt that made her feel as though she was out of time and not linked to reality.

Still, Gangu managed to find a glimmer of bravery in the middle of the waves of sadness that threatened to overtake her. Since Vikram had no other family, she realised she had to be strong. She started the difficult task of arranging preparations for his body to be at home with a heavy heart and shaking hands.

Gangu, despite her grief, carefully followed the required steps, propelled by an inner power she was unaware she had. Although her friends and coworkers came together to support and aid her, the weight of the loss seemed very personal and alienating. Her nephew from Mysore came immediately and took the reigns.

Gangu was motivated by her love and sense of responsibility for Vikram to get through the bureaucratic maze. She was aware of her obligation to preserve his memory. Despite her heartbreak and sorrow, she decided to see this last journey through, soothed by the knowledge that she was keeping her last pledge to him.

It took two difficult days to finish the bureaucratic procedures. At last, Air India carrier returned Vikram's remains to India. In the meantime, arrangements for his funeral ceremonies were painstakingly made in Bombay. Vikram's body reached Bombay early on the third day after his death, and friends and relatives gathered to say their final goodbyes. In a heartfelt and sorrowful homage, the city that had seen their shared existence now gave him one last hug.

The instant Gangu realised her beloved Vikram was going to leave her forever, her world fell apart. She was consumed by a deep sadness that seemed to last for years. She would see the sight of Vikram's lifeless body in her mind's vision every day. Vikram had spent 54 years by Gangu's side, a lifetime of memories that suddenly seemed like a weighty load of grief. She felt the sting of his absence all the time, a painful reminder of their close relationship.

He made her destitute over night when ever sge closed her eyes she could see tongues of fire dancing around her! She was in the middle that was the agony and turmoil.

# CHAPTER THIRTY-FIVE

# Gangu's Life after Vikram's Death

Gangu was sucked into deep grief and sadness upon Vikram's passing. She was full of hopelessness and a sense that everything that made her existence had been taken away. She was often struck by the joyous memories of Vikram, which brought back memories of their past happiness. Gangu's life has become a very turbulent and unpredictable journey due to the harsh touch of fate.

After the tragic death of Vishal, Vikram had been Gangu's ray of hope. Once again, with his constant love and support, he had helped her see the purpose of life and led her out of the darkness. The world appeared much colder and lonelier now that Vikram was gone. Nevertheless, Gangu found comfort in the lovely moments they had spent together.

From the year 2019 to 2021 Gangu was away from the world. Meanwhile, she has sold the businesses and other properties located at Mysore. The days were going

on Gangu won't find any hope of to resume back to life. Fortunately, on one final day, Gangu decided staying home and being isolated from the world wouldn't be working.

But once Vikram passed away suddenly, things drastically changed. Vikram's whole assets, which he had carefully gathered over the years, were finally given to Gangu. It was a sizeable sum, evidence of Vikram's accomplishments, perseverance, and hard work.

Gangu was committed to using this newfound authority to uphold Vikram's memory. Even though she was grieving, she decided to manage the assets sensibly so that Vikram's hard-earned money would keep having a good influence.

Gangu has always been a careful mother, respecting her child's independence. She thought it was best to let them handle their finances and possessions independently of her. Gangu was happy that her child could support themselves and never tried to dictate to them what to do with their money.

Gangu was a self-sufficient, determined lady who always took pleasure in her capacity to support herself. After years of assiduity, tenacity, and commitment, she had accumulated a sizeable fortune. Her wealth was more than enough to cover all of her expenses and guarantee her comfortable survival.

In addition, Gangu inherited a sizable portion of Vikram's fortune upon his demise. Gangu was highly engaged in philanthropic activities even before his death. She has been a committed Lions Club member for about thirty years, giving her time and money to several charitable initiatives. Regretfully, she had to resign from her active participation owing to her deteriorating health.

Even after this disappointment, Gangu didn't waver in her dedication to helping others. She concluded that carrying on their philanthropic heritage would be the finest use of the riches Vikram had left behind. Gangu thought that by giving this money out in Vikram's honour to worthy charities, his legacy would live on forever. She believed that by serving others, she was paying tribute to Vikram's spirit and making sure that his generosity and kindness would continue to influence the lives of those they touched.

With Vikram's death, Gangu was left alone at home. She had to make a difficult choice since the empty house and stillness became unbearable for her. She decided to relocate to an elderly residence in South India, a location that contained many of her most treasured childhood memories. Gangu was determined to locate a suitable place, so she contacted a number of her relatives and asked for help finding a trustworthy assisted living facility. She was disappointed that no one volunteered to assist her. Gangu realised that going back to the South might not be the best decision after all due to the lack of support and the uncaring attitude of her family.

Gangu thought about her predicament and concluded that finding a house nearer Mumbai would have greater significance. She had lived in the city for a long time and had benefited greatly from it, including opportunities, friendships, and a feeling of community. She felt that remaining close to Mumbai would enable her to carry out her charity endeavours in a community. Gangu set out to find a decent senior living facility close to Mumbai.

Gangu's enthusiastic participation in the Dignity Foundation, particularly during the delightful Chai-Masti sessions, prompted a brief interest in its wider range of lifestyle programmes. This led her to extensively peruse the foundation's website in an attempt to find out more about its offerings. Gangu was drawn more and more to the foundation's dedication to enhancing elderly adults' lives with a variety of activities, healthcare assistance, and a friendly environment as she read through programme descriptions and testimonies.

Gangu made the deeply felt choice to move into the Dignity Lifestyle Foundation after giving it some thought. The idea of living somewhere that reflected her ideals of respect, community, and overall health struck a deep chord with her. It signified more than simply a move, but also the continuance of her busy, rewarding life in a caring community. Gangu welcomed this new chapter with hope and purpose, knowing that the Dignity Lifestyle Foundation would give her the stability, comfort, and peace she needed.

Before shifting to dignity Gangu sold the house of Bombay. It was a terrible experience for Gangu as it took 53 years to set up the house. The flat was well furnished, and decorated with premium electronic gadgets and unique masterpieces from all over the world. At the time of selling the flat, she sold the flat with all the items. Few of the showpieces and souvenirs Gangu took with her at Dignity. She had a trip to Kashmir and it was the last trip she had after landing in Dignity Lifestyle Foundation.

Gangu had never expected to find herself at Dignity, despite being a frequent visitor and attending numerous activities over the years. One day, in joking, Gangu told Vikram, "When I grow old, you'll have to shift me to an old age home."

Vikram, always ready with a humorous comeback, made fun back, "Sure, just let me know when you're ready to leave.

They will ring me one day and say, 'Come and take your mother away.' And there you'll be, establishing a gang with all the others, laughing and raising a noise!" Vikram added.

They both laughed at the concept, seeing Gangu and her joyful circle of old comrades defying prejudices and living life with joy. Little did they know that these lighthearted interactions would become treasured memories, sewn into the fabric of their relationship. As years passed, their banter continued to lighten their days, reminding them that laughing has no age limit and that dignity can be found in the most unexpected places.

# CHAPTER THIRTY-SIX

# Twist of Life— Cancer

Before landing to the dignity while packing the luggage Gangu started getting cramps. Gangu just thought it was due to the tiredness of extreme work. Her body was giving scary signals and she refused them all. Suddenly one day Gangu started bleeding. Somewhere Gangu something scary was happening inside her as her period had stopped long back. At the age of eighty, it was strange to have a period.

Anyways Gangu went down managing somehow and thought as she reached dignity she would inform them. Within a few days after settling in dignity, Gangu informed them that they took them to the reputed hospital and consulted the issue with the gynaecologist.

The gynaecologist was doubtful that she might develop cancer but due to her age factor, she couldn't give her any medicine either.

Suddenly, Gangu would find the clots of blood going on continuously. It was becoming very difficult for Ganga to carry on. By the end of the evening, the situation got worse. It was the scariest day for Gangu as the intercom was not working. Gangu just felt helpless. She do not have anybody's contact number. But fortunately, she had the contact number of the manager of Dignity. She informed the manager of the problem.

As soon as she connected the call the nurses came and contacted the doctor who was in Pune. They were helpless; we couldn't do anything they told to Gangu. Then after a lot of discussion, the doctor suggest an injection to Gangu.

Before giving the injection, the doctor approached Gangu with a serious look and explained its significance. "You must sign an undertaking," he stated kindly but firmly. "This document states that should any complications arise post-injection, you acknowledge and accept full responsibility."

Gangu, with a cool and determined expression, replied, favourable, doctor. I will provide you with written approval."

After the formalities were done, the injection was delivered. For five precious hours, the bleeding stopped, providing a brief sensation of comfort and optimism. However, as the minutes passed, the reprieve became short. The bleeding returned, unaffected by the prior action, casting a shadow of anxiety once more.

Gangu stayed strong throughout, her courage undiminished, ready to confront whatever obstacles awaited her with unwavering tenacity.

The next day, the doctor returned from Pune and said, "We cannot administer another injection; the risk is simply too great."

Gangu stared the doctor directly in the eye and stated, "Doctor, even if it means I die, I can't take this constant bleeding any longer. I am prepared to provide you with written consent.

Her words hung in the air, a monument to her unwavering spirit and drive to find relief at whatever cost.

Gangu received the same injection twice. However, this time, the bleeding remained despite the doctor's attempts. Feeling powerless and unsure of what to do next, the doctor approached Gangu with a sorrowful heart.

"You should be taken to the hospital," the doctor said softly.

Despite her frail condition, Gangu retorted with conviction, "How can I possibly be moved to the hospital in this state?" I am bleeding profusely. "An ambulance cannot handle this situation."

Gangu thought immediately and offered, "You could speak with my gynaecologist. She's treated me before and may know what to do."

The doctor hesitated before making the call.

Gangu gave over her medical file and claimed, "Everything is here, even her phone number. "Please call her."

Her cry hung in the air, a mix of desperation and optimism, imploring the doctor to reach out and find a cure.

Finally, Gangu, in a tired but determined voice, asked the doctor, "Please dial the number for me, and I will speak with her myself." Relentlessly, the doctor made the call and eventually spoke with the gynaecologist.

After hearing the scenario, the gynaecologist reacted with a sorrowful heart, "There is no need to bring her to me. It is verified confirmed Milinenat , and given her age, there is nothing that can be done."

As this disappointing news was communicated, Gangu intervened from the background with a determined say: "Please, ask her if there is anything that can be done to stop the bleeding." If the bleeding stops, I'll be able to get on with my life. "That's all I need."

Her words rang with a mix of despair and hope, as she sought only one reprieve to continue her struggle.

The gynaecologist firmly informed the doctor, "Tell the patient there is no cure." The only alternative is this tablet, which is like a gamble. "If it works, it is a blessing."

Gangu, with steadfast resolution, consented to follow the gynaecologist's treatment plan. She started with three tablets per day for the first month, then reduced to two tablets per day for the second month, one tablet per day for the next month, and ultimately stopped taking the medicine completely.

It was nothing short of miraculous—despite all odds, the tablets began to work their magic on Gangu. She surpassed expectations at a time when many predicted the worst. Gangu was weak and lost weight at first, but her health improved. Luckily Gangu found a a doctor at Dignity Lifestyle Foundation he suggested that her cancer surgery be performed. Recently her surgery has been done successfully and she is improving. Big relief to her. The doctor who was God sent thanks to him and God for helping. She gradually acquired strength. Her recovery effectiveness of medical assistance.

Gangu emerged from the shadows of disease with tenacity and the assistance of her healthcare team, exemplifying optimism and determination in the face of adversity. Her astonishing transformation from near-despair to fresh health amazed everyone who observed it. But she has to be very careful.

*Don't be scared of death it will happen to everyone,*
*You are just powerless of how much you will live in this world,*
*Stop thinking that you can't control,*
*Love your life and be grateful for all.*

*Tribal village distribution of sarees*

*Tribal village distribution of vessels*

*Tribal village borewell pooja before starting*

*Villages thanking for borewell*

# CHAPTER THIRTY-SEVEN

# Found Peace— Present life

The journey of life is fundamentally unpredictable, with twists and turns around every bend. Gangu views problems as the cornerstone of her character, rather than a cause of dread. She thrives on conquering problems, exemplifying resilience and strength. Bravery is her ornament, representing her unyielding commitment. She confronts obstacles front-on, frequently making them appear trivial in comparison.

Gangu endured a difficult eight decades. Each year brought its own set of challenges, but she faced them with determination and courage. She did not have any kind of support; she proceeded on her own, depending on her inner strength and tenacity. She forged her way with pure strength and unwavering determination, demonstrating that genuine grit and perseverance can conquer even the most formidable circumstances.

Success is a concept with several definitions. Gangu defines success by her independence, whereas others measure it by wealth or popularity. She has attained a level of self-reliance that many strive for but few reach. Her tale exemplifies the strength of resilience, demonstrating that with enough persistence, one can overcome any challenge and take their proper position in the world.

Losing her loved ones paused her for a while, but she rose from her pain with the vibrant colours of a rainbow. Many people felt she was lost and beyond repair, but the Creator had other plans for her. He gave her a newfound purpose, a new life committed to serving others. Gangu, tough and resolute, welcomed this second opportunity with an open heart and unflinching resolve.

Gangu, determined to make a significant difference, committed to donating her money to philanthropic causes for the rest of her life. Her experiences have taught her the virtue of compassion and the significance of contributing to the community. She understood the challenges of people less fortunate and had a strong desire to alleviate their pain. Her charity was more than just donating money; it was about offering hope, assistance, and a brighter future for people in need.

Her willingness to donate her money to charity exemplified her humility and kindness. Gangu felt that genuine riches rested not in worldly belongings, but in the power to positively impact the lives of others. She committed herself to this cause with the same tenacity that had gotten her through her worst days. Her philanthropic efforts became a source of hope and inspiration, illustrating the transformational power of compassion and the resilience of the human spirit.

Gangu's acts demonstrated that even in the face of severe loss and tragedy, one may emerge stronger and more determined than before. Her life became a living example of the human spirit's resiliency and limitless capacity for love and giving. Gangu's path, distinguished by her unrelenting devotion to philanthropy, is a striking reminder that even in the worst of times, the most meaningful and enduring gifts to mankind may emerge.

Soon after her bleeding stopped and her condition improved, she set out on her objective to become a provider in society. She started giving ration to the Dignity Life Style personnel. The amount of supplies she gave was enormous, enough to last two months. Everyone was grateful for her efforts, as the rations allowed the personnel to focus on their work without thinking about their fundamental necessities. This act of generosity demonstrated not just her resilience, but also her dedication to helping her community in times of need.

She then moved her focus to neighbourhoods near the Dignity Lifestyle. She had already provided clothing and vessels to the remote people. However, due to a major language barrier, Gangu was unable to completely understand their most important demands. Fortunately, she met a boy who could speak on her behalf and bridge the gap between her and the locals.

The residents have not seen a steady source of water in years. They had to go vast distances to get just one bucket of water, which was a difficult and time-consuming chore. The prospect of arranging for a borewell appeared practically unachievable owing to the technical and financial difficulties involved.

Despite these challenges, Gangu remained determined. Through sheer determination, she learned that some local people had successfully erected a borewell. Gangu seized this chance and asked them for advice and counsel. She requested their assistance in locating a water source in the community and constructing a borewell.

Her efforts to comprehend the villagers' suffering, as well as her attempt to ensure a sustainable water supply, greatly improved their living conditions. Gangu's persistent dedication to improving the lives of people in need. She sometimes sponsors day food for patients and gives them funds.

Gangu built the borewell after much hardship and patience. The folks were dancing joyfully and expressing deep thanks. They applauded Gangu for her noble cause, recognising her efforts to alleviate their long-standing water crisis, which had impacted generations. The borewell is now fully functioning and provides the hamlet with much-needed water supplies. This achievement was a huge milestone, altering the villagers' everyday lives and assuring the community's stable water supply. Gangu's devotion and hard work resulted in a remarkable improvement, winning her the affection and respect of everyone in the town.

In addition to her work in the community, Gangu has made many major gifts on Vikram's behalf. Her major achievements included co-sponsoring a ward at the Shanti Avedna Sadan, a well-known hospice for terminal cancer patients in Bandra. This institution provides care and comfort to individuals in the terminal stages of cancer, and Gangu's assistance has improved the quality of life for many patients at difficult times.Sometimes she sponsor day food to patience and contributes Corpus Fund.

Gangu also donated to the Tata Memorial Hospital, which is one of the country's leading cancer treatment facilities. She contributed money expressly for chemotherapy treatments, allowing more people to get this life-saving medication. Due to her restricted mobility, hospital workers gladly collected the donations from her house, demonstrating their gratitude for her ongoing devotion to cancer patients.

Gangu's gifts demonstrate his deep compassion and devotion to alleviating the pain of others. By donating to these prestigious institutions, she has helped to provide critical medical treatment and assistance to individuals in need. Her charity initiatives continue to make a real impact in the lives of many people.

Following these charitable activities, Vikram devoted himself to tourism. To encourage academic success in this field, Gangu funded two gold medals for excellent Garware Institute master's and bachelor's students. Her sponsorship intended to encourage and reward people who displayed great aptitude and devotion to their tourism studies.

Gangu attended the Garware Institute's convocation ceremonies for the past two years, personally presenting these distinguished honours. Her attendance at these occasions provided a great sense of respect and inspiration to the recipients and the whole student population. Gangu's ability to travel was severely hampered following her cancer diagnosis. As a result, she was unable to continue attending in-person convocation ceremonies.

Despite her physical disappearance, Gangu's legacy of promoting tourism education endured. Her efforts continued to motivate pupils to strive for greatness and pursue their goals with zeal. The gold medals she sponsored continue to represent her unwavering dedication to promoting academic performance and professional development in the tourist industry.

Gangu has also been a strong supporter of the Saint Catherine Welfare Institute in Bandra, which focuses on educating disadvantaged children. She makes considerable gifts to this institute twice a year, ensuring that the youngsters have the resources they need to further their education and build a brighter future. Gangu would personally visit the Saint Catherine Welfare before becoming active, to oversee her donations and observe the good impact of her assistance. She has given education endoement funds for scholarships.

Gangu has actively participated in tribal community development initiatives in addition to her employment at the Saint Catherine Welfare Institute. She has worked with the same agency to address tribal children's educational needs, seeing the importance of education in breaking the cycle of poverty and empowering communities.

Gangu has gone above and above in her support for our cause, financing the education of 100 youngsters from the first standard to twelve standard. This sponsorship guarantees that these children have access to ongoing and high-quality education, equipping them with the skills and information needed to succeed in life. Her unrelenting attention to both children's welfare and the upliftment of tribal communities demonstrates her deep commitment to bringing about long-term constructive social change. Gangu's continued efforts have impacted numerous lives and inspired others to help people in need. Dignity Lifestyle has started a stay for lower-income people as Garima Ghar. She has contributed a good amount for Garima Ghar. Recently she has contributed to Mouth and Foot painting artists located in Andheri for uniquely abled artists.

Gangu is a firm believer in the profound beauty of life, seeking comfort in moments of peace and thankfulness for the benefits she has received. Through the highs and lows, she accepts both happy and terrible days as necessary elements of life's journey. Rather than remaining on regrets, Gangu sees each event as an opportunity for inspiration and progress.

According to her, life is full of lessons and opportunities for personal growth. Each hardship she faces serves as a stepping stone to greater resilience, while times of joy and peace remind her of the fundamental beauty of life. Gangu's viewpoint is a light of optimism, inspiring others to treasure every moment, learn from misfortune, and nurture thankfulness for the abundance of life. Her story exemplifies the transformational power of perspective, demonstrating how accepting life in its fullness may result in tremendous inner peace and fulfilment.

www.ingramcontent.com/pod-product-compliance
Lightning Source LLC
Chambersburg PA
CBHW031139130726
47988CB00006B/2444